Back Roads Bicycling...

...in Bucks County, Pa.

By Catherine D. Kerr

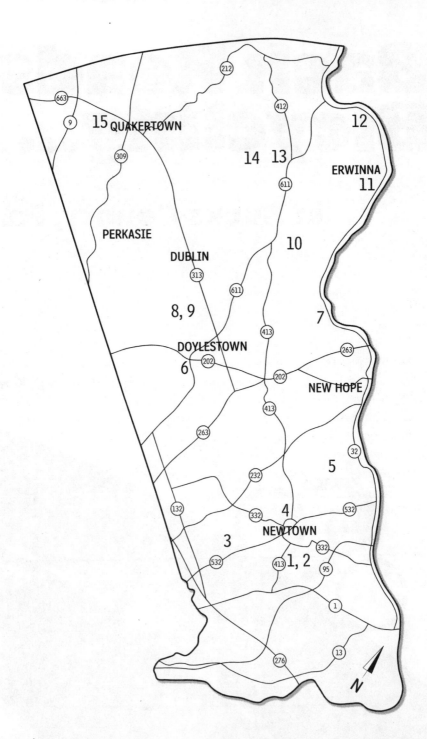

Back Roads Bicycling...

...in Bucks County, Pa.

By Catherine D. Kerr

Please ride cautiously! **No matter how carefully a bicycling route is planned, it is impossible to eliminate all potential hazards or to foresee changes in road conditions. Even on bike paths and back roads, bicycle riding always involves a certain degree of risk.**

Bicyclists should observe the usual guidelines for safe cycling, including:

- **Wear a helmet.**

- **Stay to the right and ride single file.**

- **Take care to avoid road hazards such as potholes.**

- **Always watch out for cars, even where there doesn't appear to be much traffic.**

- **Don't go so fast you lose control of your bicycle.**

- **Yield to pedestrians, especially when riding along mixed-use paths.**

ISBN 0-9652733-2-6

FREEWHEELING PRESS
P.O. Box 540
Lahaska PA 18931

http://www.voicenet.com/~ckerr
e-mail: ckerr@voicenet.com

PRINTED IN CANADA

Contents

Thanks!

This book is dedicated to my parents, who probably didn't think things would turn out this way (see letter from Santa below), with much love to Chris, Nick, and Kate, who live with me and my projects as they come together.

Many cyclists helped me in ways that ranged from suggesting good biking roads in Bucks County to providing detailed cue sheets, and I thank them all.

NORTH POLE-SANTA LAND
December 17, 1958.

DEAR CATHERINE MARY:

I have just learned from one of my helpers at the NORTH POLE that you would like a two wheel bike for Christmas. Santa is very sorry to tell you that he will be unable to grant your wish, as he feels it might be a dangerous gift if given to you at this time. Knowing you to be very thoughtful, and a sensible girl, I am sure you would not want to cause mamma or daddy any worry, nor would you want to place the blame on Santa Claus for giving you the bike, should you ever have an accident.

May I ask that you let me know quickly as possible what I can bring for you in place of the bike, and in the meantime I must rejoin my helpers, in order that all of the presents be delivered on time for Christmas.

Love to all.

Santa Claus

Introduction

When my first collection of bicycle tours was published in 1996, I was thrilled by the enthusiastic praise it received from other cyclists. People told me they appreciated *The Back Roads Bike Book's* careful selection of routes, which showcase the wonderful scenery near my home in New Hope, Pa. They liked the step-by-step route directions and the detailed maps. They were also glad to have listings for places to buy refreshments and points of interest along the way.

Steady sales of the book confirmed that it was filling a definite need, but soon people were telling me they wanted more. The first book concentrated on relatively short and easy rides near the Delaware River from Washington Crossing to Frenchtown. Couldn't I put together something that would include some longer and more challenging routes, as well as covering a broader area?

I could, and I did—this volume is the result. Although it largely avoids the heavily developed southern part of Bucks County, *Back Roads Bicycling in Bucks County, Pa.* has rides almost everywhere else. Its featured routes range from the easy one-mile bike path in Core Creek Park to a 47-mile loop that takes Eagle Road nearly to the top of Jericho Mountain, climbing about 240 feet in half a mile. Naturally, there's plenty in between those two extremes. Cyclists at every level should be able to find a ride that's just right in this volume.

Good maps and clear directions remain at the heart of the book. The maps are designed to provide enough information to allow you to make short departures from the planned route or to find your way again if you happen to make a wrong turn, although they don't include every street. Like its predecessor, *Back Roads Bicycling in Bucks County, Pa.* also includes listings for places to eat and things to do along each route. This time, I've also tried to provide a choice of detours that can make an easy ride more interesting for experienced cyclists or tame challenging routes to make them more accessible.

The layout of the maps and directions might seem a bit odd, but the sideways design is intended to make it easier to stop and consult these sections while you are on the road. When the cues run to more than one page, the maps are repeated so you can always view both map and directions without having to flip back and forth in the book. And cyclists who use the type of handlebar bag that has a clear map case on top might wish to actually remove pages from the book and carry them in the map case.

Because the rides vary so widely in distance and terrain, each one is rated as easy, medium or difficult. I thought these ratings would be useful even though I realize the potential problems. I know that "easy" or "difficult" is relative when it comes to cycling. Some riders will think my medium rides are easy, while others will find them much too hard. Basically, only those routes that are shorter than ten miles with no more than one or two significant hills are classified here as easy. Difficult rides include a number of steep hills or other conditions that require some particular skill to ride. Everything else—and that includes most of the routes in the book—is in the middle category. In calculating distances, I relied on a combination of car and bicycle odometers and maps. These figures are provided for your guidance but they are estimates only, and I cannot guarantee their accuracy.

Please pay careful attention to the safety suggestions listed on the second page of this book. I've tried hard to be selective about which roads to include here, avoiding those with narrow shoulders and lots of traffic, but bicycling always involves a certain degree of risk. Also, continuing development has led to increased car traffic all over Bucks County, and choosing the right time of day to ride can make a big difference in how many cars you'll see on the road. Generally, early week-

The bike path at Peace Valley Park

end mornings are the best times to ride, while the period from 3 to 6 P.M. weekdays is probably the worst.

The appendix includes tourism information for visitors to Bucks County, as well as listings for bike shops, rentals and clubs. The opportunity to participate in this section of the book was open to any shop or club that returned a completed information sheet. These listings are provided as a convenience to cyclists; they should not be interpreted as a recommendation against any shop or club not included here.

Finally, I wish you all happy cycling—and I hope you have as much fun using this book as I've had putting it together!

Catherine D. Kerr

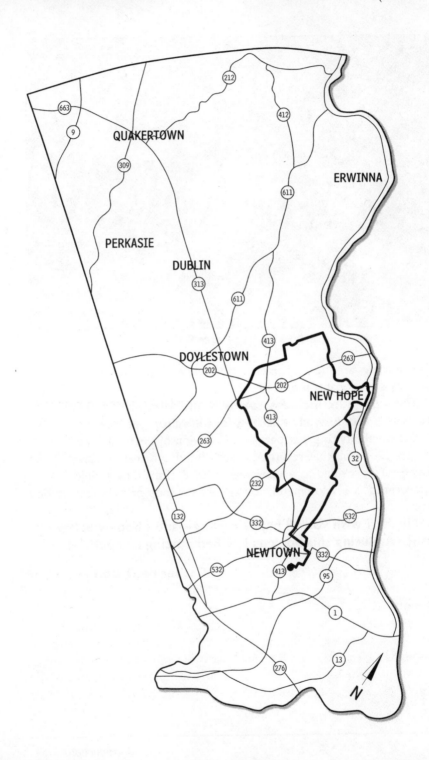

The sampler

Distance: 47.1 miles
Rating: Difficult
Start: Core Creek Park

I think of this ride as a Bucks County sampler because it provides an excellent introduction to the pleasures of bicycling here. After fifty miles of riding past rolling farmland, shaded woods, the Delaware River, panoramic views of distant hills, dignified country estates, a busy tourist town, a historic 300-year-old borough—not to mention a few developments so new they haven't planted the grass yet—you'll understand why so many cyclists come to Bucks County to ride.

The route also includes one really tough climb, along with directions for a detour around it. If your preferred style of cycling is a little more relaxed, though, don't worry. No other ride in this book is as long or as difficult as this one. Bucks County has roads and bike trails for riders at every level, and I've tried to provide a little something for everyone in this book.

This ride begins at Core Creek Park, a county park off Route 413 just south of Newtown. (See page 15 for more information on the park, including a close-up map.) It's a big park with all the usual amenities: rest rooms, picnic areas, playgrounds, etc. It also has a very nice one-mile bike path along the shore of Lake Luxembourg. For this ride, you can leave

Variations:

Avoid crossing Jericho Mountain on Eagle Rd. Follow the planned route to mile 8.0, where you turn right onto Eagle Rd. Make the next left onto Pineville Rd. From there, make the second right onto Buckmanville Rd. When Buckmanville ends at Street Rd., turn left onto Street. Make the first right onto Lurgan Rd. and pick up the main directions again at mile 10.4 by turning left onto Van Sant Rd. This detour shortens the ride by about a mile.

Shorten the ride by parking at Magill's Hill Park on Chapel Rd. at Route 32 north of New Hope. For a 28-mile ride, you can start at mile 16.4 in the planned route. Follow the directions to the bridge in Wycombe at mile 33.9. From the bridge, go straight onto Township Line Rd. When Township Line ends at a stop sign, cross Route 413 carefully and walk your bike across the front of the Pineville Tavern. Turn left onto Pine La. When Pine ends at a stop sign, cross Route 232 and continue straight ahead on Pineville Rd. Make the first left onto Buckmanville Rd. When Buckmanville ends at a stop sign, turn left onto Street Rd. Make the first right onto Lurgan Rd. Make the first left onto Van Sant Rd. and follow the original directions from mile 10.4 back to Magill's Hill.

your car at any of the Core Creek parking areas; there's one conveniently located just inside the entrance to the park from Tollgate Road.

The inspiration for this ride comes from a slightly longer route put together by Lou Spadafora, a C-Quad Cycling Club member. My version includes a few small modifications intended mostly to avoid some of the busier roads included in Lou's route, which can be found in its original form on the World Wide Web at

http://cquad.home.mindspring.com/romo.html

Once you leave Core Creek Park, the first few miles of the ride take you around the edge of Newtown. From there you'll head uphill toward Jericho Mountain, which tops out at 442 feet. That makes it only half the size of the highest peaks in Bucks County, and Eagle Road itself doesn't quite make it to 442, but it does rise 240 feet in just over a half a mile. The actual crossing of the peak comes on Eagle Road between Pineville

The bridge from New Hope to Lambertville

Road and Thompson Mill Road, but you can avoid this extreme hill by taking the detour described on the preceding page.

Finding Stoney Hill Road at mile 14.5 is tricky because Stoney Hill is so small it could be mistaken for a driveway. If you find yourself crossing a stream and some railroad tracks, you've missed the turn. Stoney Hill leads into Mechanic Street, which takes you right into New Hope. This is a good place to take a break and enjoy the shops and restaurants. (You'll find several suggestions for places to eat at the end of this chapter, but there are many others—look around until you find something you like.)

Leaving New Hope, the route climbs back out onto a series of country roads, which bring you back to civilization (in the form of new development) when you hit Eagle Road again. South Eagle Road runs through a shopping area with several places to eat, including a bagel shop, a hoagie shop, and a sit-down restaurant named Goodnoe's, which used to be practically the only thing here. There's also a Wendy's where South Eagle ends at Washington Street.

From there, you'll ride through Newtown on Washington Street to retrace the route to Core Creek Park from Terry Road. Newtown is a pleasant place to wander if you still have the stamina; check out the historic district, which dates back to the time of William Penn.

Good to know:

Core Creek Park, 901 E. Bridgetown Pike, Langhorne, (215) 757-0571 (Bucks County Parks Dept.). Boat rentals, ball fields, basketball courts, picnicking, tennis, rest rooms, equestrian trails.

Newtown:

Bagel Junction, 2826 S. Eagle Rd., Newtown, (215) 968-9795. In the same part of the shopping center as Genuardi's.

Goodnoe Farm Dairy Bar, 298 N. Sycamore St. (just west of S. Eagle Rd. on the edge of the shopping area), Newtown, (215) 968-3875. A family restaurant that is famous for its ice cream.

Lee's Hoagie House, 2810 S. Eagle Rd., Newtown, (215) 860-8330. In the same part of the shopping center as Genuardi's.

Pizza Hut, 2050 S. Eagle Rd, Newtown, (215) 968-6040. Behind Wendy's at Swamp Rd.

Wendy's, 2000 S. Eagle Rd., Newtown, (215) 968-4579. At the Swamp Rd. end of the shopping center.

New Hope:

New Hope Village Store, 16 S. Main St., New Hope, (215) 862-5485. Sandwiches, ice cream, drinks, and other takeout food.

Golden Pump, 4 S. Main St., New Hope, (215) 862-5116. A sit-down, diner-type restaurant.

Cafe Lulu's, 110 S. Main St., New Hope, (215) 862-3222. Outdoor seating available.

New York Cafe and Delicatessen, 12 W. Bridge St., New Hope, (215) 862-1755. Near the corner of Bridge and Main.

Solebury Friends Meeting on Sugan Road

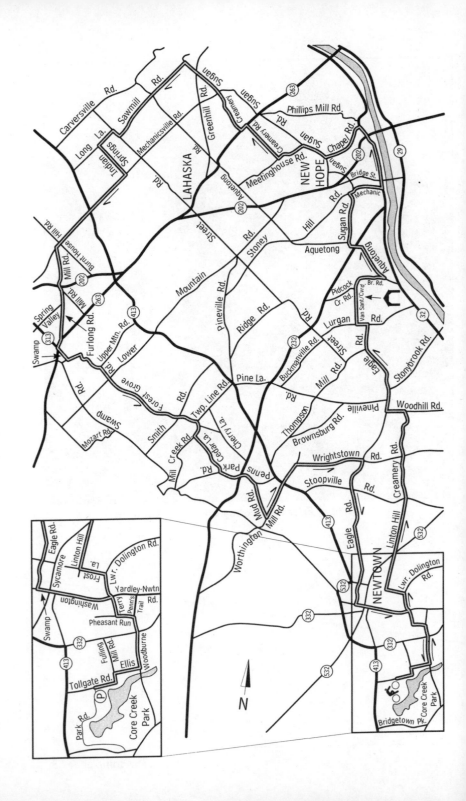

Directions:

0.0 Turn **right** from the park road onto Tollgate Rd.

0.3 At the stop sign, turn **left** onto Fulling Mill Rd.

0.5 At the stop sign, turn **right** onto Ellis Rd.

0.9 When Ellis ends at a traffic signal, turn **left** onto Woodbourne Rd.

1.5 At the traffic signal, cross Route 332 (carefully—it's a four-lane road here) and continue **straight** ahead on Penn's Trail.

1.8 Make the first **left** onto Pheasant Run.

2.2 At the stop sign, turn **right** onto Terry Rd.

2.4 At the traffic light, cross Yardley-Newtown Rd. and continue **straight** ahead on Lower Dolington Rd.

2.8 At the top of the hill, turn **left** onto Frost La.

3.3 At the stop sign, turn **right** onto Linton Hill Rd. (to the left, the sign says Lincoln Dr.).

5.5 Cross Stoopville Rd. and continue **straight** ahead on Creamery Rd.

7.6 When Creamery ends at a stop sign, turn **left** onto Woodhill Rd.

8.0 At the stop sign, turn **right** onto Eagle Rd.

8.5 At the intersection with Stonybrook Rd., bear to the **left** to continue on Eagle. The big climb is just ahead.

9.1 You've reached the top of the hill!

10.2 When Eagle ends at a stop sign, turn **left** onto Lurgan Rd.

10.4 Turn **right** onto Van Sant Rd. (It becomes Covered Bridge Rd.)

12.1 When Covered Bridge ends at a stop sign, turn **left** onto Aquetong Rd.

13.2 At the stop sign, cross Route 232 (Windy Bush Rd.) and continue **straight** ahead on Aquetong.

13.4 When Aquetong goes off to the left, continue **straight** onto Sugan Rd.

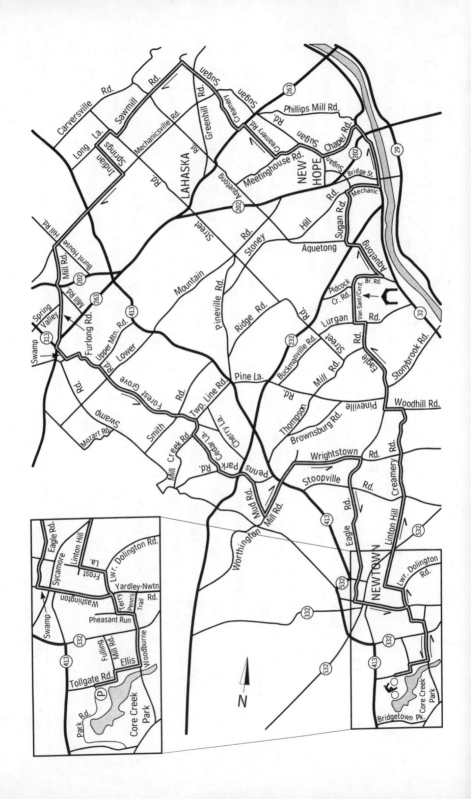

14.5 When Sugan seems to end at a stop sign, turn **right.**

14.5 Immediately after the turn from Sugan, bear **right** onto Stoney Hill Rd. (This small road, which leads into Mechanic St., is easy to miss.)

15.2 Take care approaching the entrance to Village II. Watch for cars turning left (across your path) into this development.

15.4 At a stop sign just after you cross the Delaware Canal, turn **left** onto Route 32 (S. Main St.).

15.6 At the traffic signal at Bridge St., continue **straight** ahead on N. Main.

16.1 Pass under Route 202, watching out for cars using the highway's on and off ramps.

16.4 Turn **left** onto Chapel Rd. (Magill's Hill Park is on the left here.)

17.5 When Chapel ends at a stop sign, turn **right** onto Sugan Rd.

18.1 Across from Solebury Friends Meeting, turn **left** onto Meetinghouse Rd.

18.7 Turn **right** onto Creamery Rd.

19.7 Turn **left** onto Route 263.

19.8 Make the next **right** back onto Creamery Rd.

20.9 At the stop sign at Mechanicsville Rd., go **straight** ahead to continue on Sugan.

21.9 Turn **left** onto Sawmill Rd.

22.9 At the stop sign, cross Aquetong Rd. and continue **straight** ahead on Sawmill.

24.1 Turn **right** onto Street Rd.

24.3 Turn **left** onto Long La.

24.7 Turn **left** onto Indian Springs Rd.

25.6 Turn **right** onto Mechanicsville.

26.8 At the traffic signal at Route 413, go **straight** ahead to continue on Mechanicsville.

27.7 Cross Burnt House Hill Rd.

27.8 Bear **left** onto Mill Rd.

28.7 At the stop sign, cross Route 202 (carefully) and continue **straight** ahead on Mill.

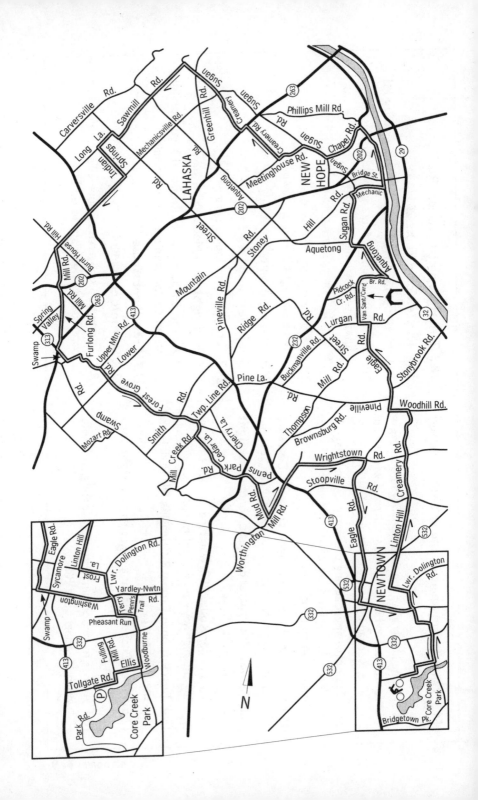

28.9 Bear **right** onto Furlong Rd.

30.0 At the stop sign, turn **right** onto Route 263.

30.1 At the traffic signal, turn **left** onto Swamp Rd.

30.4 At the stop sign, go **straight** ahead to continue on Swamp. (Ignore the sign that shows Swamp going off to the right.)

31.3 At the intersection where Upper Mountain Rd. goes straight ahead, go **right** to continue on Forest Grove Rd.

33.5 Go around the "road closed" signs at the intersection with Smith Rd. and continue **straight** ahead on Forest Grove.

33.9 Cross the bridge in Wycombe.

34.0 Turn **right** onto Mill Creek Rd.

34.3 Turn **left** onto Cedar La.

35.4 When Cedar ends at a stop sign, turn **left** onto Penns Park Rd.

35.8 At the stop sign at Route 232, cross carefully and continue **straight** ahead on Penns Park.

36.3 Turn **right** onto Mud Rd.

37.1 Turn **left** onto Worthington Mill Rd.

37.9 At the stop sign at Route 413, cross very carefully and go **straight** ahead onto Wrightstown Rd.

38.4 When Hampton Rd. goes off to the left, stay **right** to continue on Wrightstown.

39.9 Turn **right** onto Eagle Rd.

40.7 At the blinker light, cross Stoopville and continue **straight** ahead on Eagle.

42.8 At the traffic signal, cross Route 532 carefully and continue **straight** ahead on S. Eagle Rd. through the shopping center.

43.3 When S. Eagle ends at a stop sign, turn **left** onto Swamp Rd. (This becomes Washington Ave.)

43.5 At the traffic signal, cross N. Sycamore St. and continue **straight** ahead on Washington. Ride carefully through Newtown.

44.5 Turn **right** onto Terry.

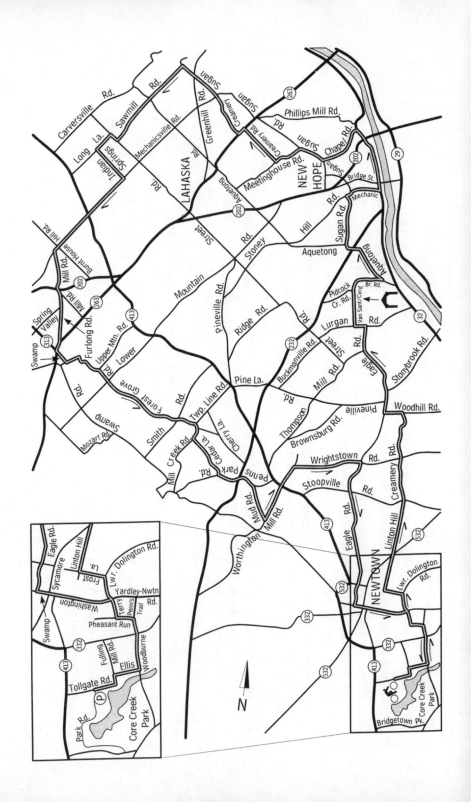

44.9 At the stop sign, turn **left** onto Pheasant Run.

45.2 At the stop sign, turn **right** onto Penn's Trail.

45.4 At the traffic signal, cross Route 332 and continue **straight** ahead on Woodbourne.

46.0 Turn **right** onto Ellis.

46.6 At the stop sign, turn **left** onto Fulling Mill. (Take care because traffic coming from your right has the right of way.)

46.8 Turn **right** onto Tollgate.

47.1 Turn **left** to return to the park.

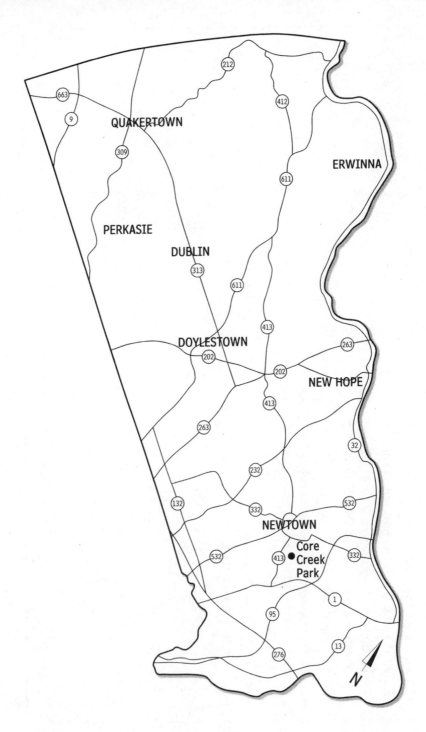

Core Creek Park

Distance: 1.0 miles
Rating: Easy
Paved bike path

Core Creek Park is probably most famous for the Christmas light show that takes place there each year, but in warmer seasons it's a wonderful place for a short, very easy bike ride along the path that skirts the shores of lovely Lake Luxembourg.

During the holiday season, for a small charge per carload (the money goes to support local charities), you can roll along the park road in your automobile admiring a series of displays outlined in bright colored lights. The show isn't particularly popular with the neighbors, mostly because of its extreme popularity with everyone else. At other times of the year, a less congested Core Creek Park is better known as a place to enjoy biking, boating, picnicking, or a romp on one of its playgrounds.

The park bike path isn't much of a challenge for experienced cyclists, but it's the perfect place to bring a beginning rider for a taste of the fun longer bike rides can be. As the map on the next page shows, the path extends from the parking lot near the northern park entrance past two other lots to join the park road near the southern end of the lake. The path itself is a mile long. Cyclists share it with pedestrians, baby strollers, inline skaters, and so forth, so it's best to use it at times when the park isn't terribly busy—a summer weekday, for example. There is a small hill

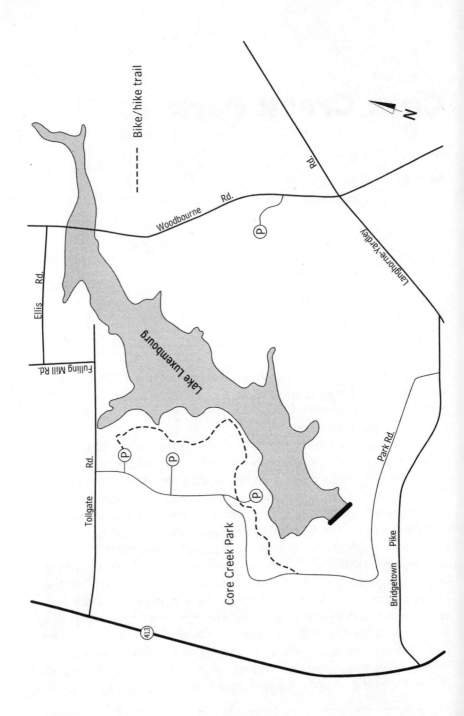

N

Bike/hike trail

Woodbourne Rd.

Langhorne-Yardley Rd.

Ellis Rd.

Fulling Mill Rd.

Lake Luxembourg

Tollgate Rd.

Park Rd.

Core Creek Park

Bridgetown Pike

413

P

P

P

P

16

at the northern end of the path, but it is otherwise mostly gently rolling. For a longer ride, you can continue on the park road to the southern entrance; you'll encounter some traffic, but it shouldn't be very heavy on a normal day.

Core Creek Park, which is a Bucks County facility, is located just east of Route 413 in Middletown Township, and it can be reached from Tollgate Road on the north or Bridgetown Pike on the south. The nearest place to look for refreshments is Newtown, just a few miles north on Route 413.

Good to know:

Core Creek Park, 901 E. Bridgetown Pike, Langhorne, (215) 757-0571 (Bucks County Parks Dept.). Boat rentals, ball fields, basketball courts, picnicking, tennis, rest rooms, equestrian trails.

For nearby food stops, see listings in Newtown on page 4.

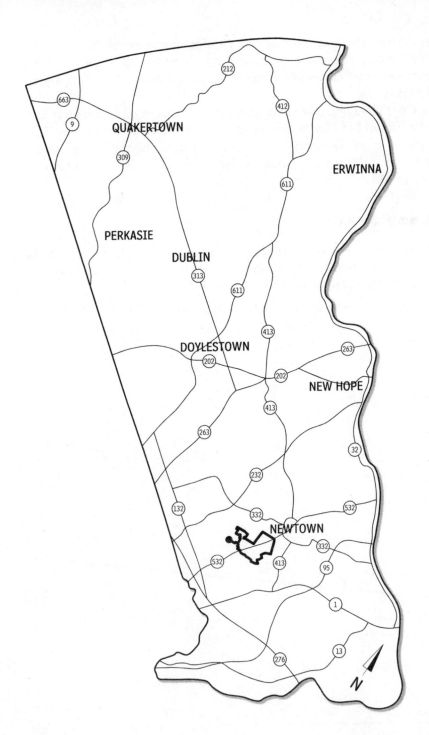

QUAKERTOWN

ERWINNA

PERKASIE

DUBLIN

DOYLESTOWN

NEW HOPE

NEWTOWN

Churchville

Distance: 10.7 miles
Rating: Easy
Start: Churchville Nature Center

The Churchville Nature Center is a real gem, an island of calm in the busy southern section of Bucks County. It's a place where you can relax on a bench by a springhouse and admire a quiet pond, or watch the comings and goings of waterfowl on the beautiful Churchville Reservoir. Nature trails spread out from the main building through a variety of environments. Best of all for anyone wishing to use the facility as home base for a bicycle trip, there are rest rooms and tables where you can enjoy a picnic lunch after your ride.

The truth is, it's not easy to find a great bike ride in Lower Bucks County. Most of the land is rather densely developed, and the roads tend to have narrow shoulders and plenty of traffic, making cycling unpleasant at best—and downright risky at worst. To be perfectly honest, this 10.7-mile route isn't likely to be anyone's pick for the best ride in this book. It is, however, one of the nicest to be had in this part of the county.

The route winds in and out of several developments in order to avoid some of the busiest streets, so close attention to the map and cue sheet is essential. The map provides enough detail to get you through these residential neighborhoods but not enough to allow you to explore them at length (not something you'd likely want to try, anyway). Cyclists might

A peaceful reflecting pond at the Churchville Nature Center

encounter some traffic on Holland Road and again on Bridgetown Pike, which is also somewhat narrow. On most of these streets, however, the largest vehicles you'll find are school buses and trucks from furniture stores making deliveries to the newer sections of the developments.

The ride begins at the parking lot of the nature center, located on Churchville Lane between Holland and Bristol roads in Northampton Township. Churchville Lane, aptly named because it does have the look and feel of a peaceful country lane, brings you to Holland Road. After a

Variations:

Avoid Bridgetown Pike. From Stoney Ford Rd. at mile 7.1, turn right instead of left onto East Holland Rd. Follow East Holland back to Vanderveer, then retrace the first part of the ride. This detour also eliminates the two significant hills on the route, on E. Holland Rd. just before Pepperell Dr. and on Heron Rd. just after the turn from Bridgetown. It creates a route that is about 12 miles long.

Ride Bridgetown Pike to Neshaminy Creek. If you're out early on a Sunday morning or some other time when traffic is minimal, turn left instead of right onto Bridgetown from Watergate Rd. at mile 7.9. Ride about a mile and a half to the pretty little bridge over Neshaminy Creek, just before Route 413, then return the same way to pick up the route.

short turn on Holland, you'll bypass a busy stretch by detouring through a development, then return briefly to Holland Road to cross the railroad right-of-way. Another spin through a development brings you to Lower Holland Road, which takes you across Holland Road and into another development. From here, it's more of the same all the way back to the nature center. Cars tend to go fast on Bridgetown Pike and there isn't much shoulder, but the traffic isn't too bad if you avoid late weekday afternoons there.

The route stays away from stores and shopping centers, but there are a couple of places nearby where you could pick up refreshments to enjoy at the end of your ride.

Good to know:

Churchville Nature Center, 501 Churchville La., Churchville, (215) 357-4005. Nature trails, special programs, rest rooms, waterfront views, picnic area.

Wawa Food Market, Holland Shopping Center (intersection of Route 532 and Holland Rd.), Holland, (215) 357-2602. Drinks, sandwiches, snacks.

Krauszer's, 295 Buck Rd. (intersection of Buck and Rocksville rds.), Holland, (215) 357-7152. A convenience store.

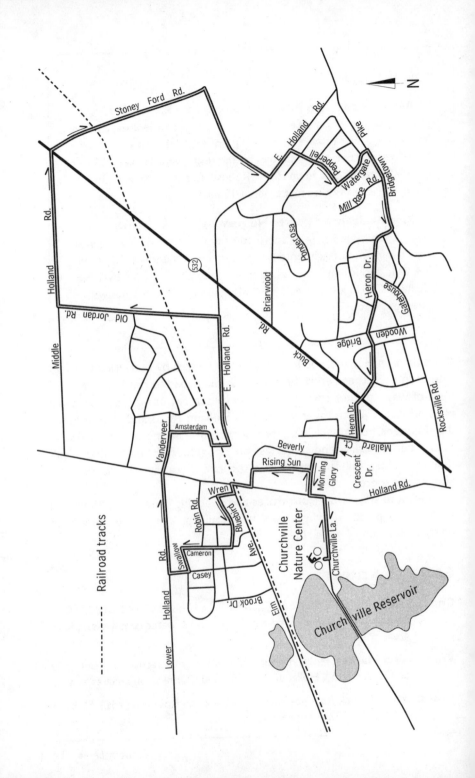

Directions:

0.0 Turn **left** out of the Churchville Nature Center onto Churchville La.

0.3 When Churchville ends at a stop sign, turn **left** onto Holland Rd.

0.4 Make the first **right** onto Morning Glory Ave.

0.5 At the stop sign, make the first **left** onto Rising Sun Ave.

0.8 When Rising Sun ends at a stop sign, turn **left** onto E. Patricia Rd.

0.9 At the stop sign, turn **right** onto Holland.

1.0 Immediately after the railroad, turn **left** onto Elm Ave.

1.1 Make the first **right** onto Wren Dr.

1.2 Turn **left** onto Bluebird Rd.

1.5 When Bluebird ends at a stop sign, turn **right** onto Cameron Rd.

1.8 When Cameron ends at a stop sign, turn **left** onto Swallow Rd.

1.9 At the stop sign, turn **right** onto Casey Rd.

2.0 At the stop sign, turn **right** onto Lower Holland Rd.

2.5 At the stop sign, go **straight** across Holland to continue on Vanderveer Ave.

2.7 At the stop sign, turn **right** onto Amsterdam Ave.

3.0 At the stop sign, turn **left** onto E. Holland Rd.

3.8 Just after Holland Jr. High School, turn **left** onto Old Jordan Rd.

4.7 At the stop sign, turn **right** onto Middle Holland Rd.

5.5 At the traffic signal, cross Route 532 (Buck Rd.) and continue **straight** ahead on Stoney Ford Rd.

7.1 At the stop sign, turn **left** onto E. Holland.

7.3 Make the first **right** onto Pepperell Dr.

7.6 When Pepperell ends at a stop sign, turn **left** onto Watergate Dr.

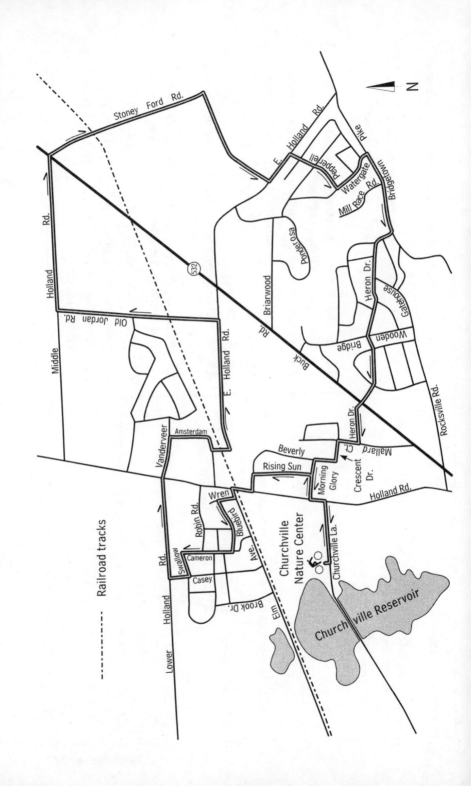

Railroad tracks

7.8 Follow the road around a curve and turn **right** onto Watergate Rd.

7.9 At the stop sign, turn **right** onto Bridgetown Pike.

8.4 Turn **right** onto Heron Rd. Continue on Heron through the development, crossing a number of small intersections.

9.4 At a stop sign, cross Route 532 carefully and continue **straight** on Heron.

9.6 When Heron ends at a stop sign, turn **right** onto Mallard Ct.

9.7 At the stop sign, turn **left** onto Crescent Dr.

9.8 At the stop sign, turn **right** onto Beverly Rd.

10.0 At the stop sign, turn **left** onto Morning Glory.

10.2 At the stop sign, turn **left** onto Holland.

10.3 Turn **right** onto Churchville.

10.7 Turn **right** into the parking lot at the Churchville Nature Center. (To see the Churchville Reservoir, ride ahead about 0.2 miles on Churchville La.)

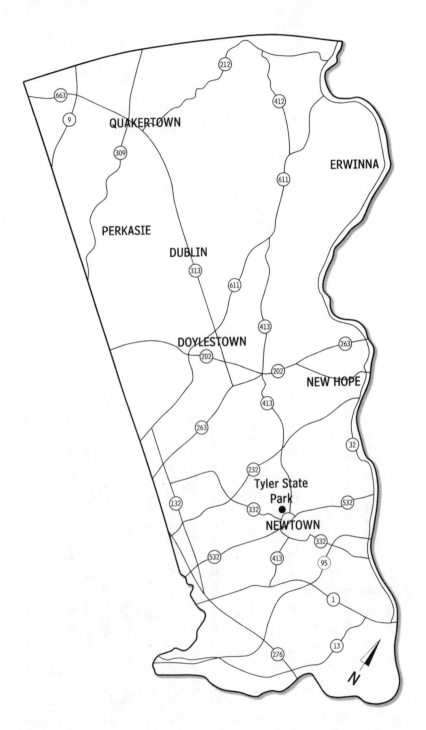

Tyler State Park

Distance: 10.5 miles
Rating: Varies
Paved bike paths

Tyler State Park is known for its rolling hills, cultivated fields, early stone farmhouses, playgrounds, and picnic areas, and it is especially popular with bicyclists because of the network of paved bike paths—10.5 miles of them—that wind along through all of this and provide some great views of the wide and scenic Neshaminy Creek.

Because much of the land in the park is quite hilly, especially on the west side of the creek, the trails are best for serious cyclists looking for places to ride away from automobile traffic. However, the Tyler Drive Trail is nearly flat for about three-quarters of a mile from the parking area near the pedestrian causeway, and this section is suitable even for small children. The view of the creek from this part of the trail is also quite nice. In fact, it's no accident that the parking lot near the causeway and the canoe rental concession is the largest, since this is arguably the prettiest part of the park.

The park headquarters is located near the main entrance from Swamp Road, at the intersection with Route 413 near Newtown. You can stop there and pick up a copy of the official park map to use in your explorations. Take special care on the winding downhills, because the bike paths

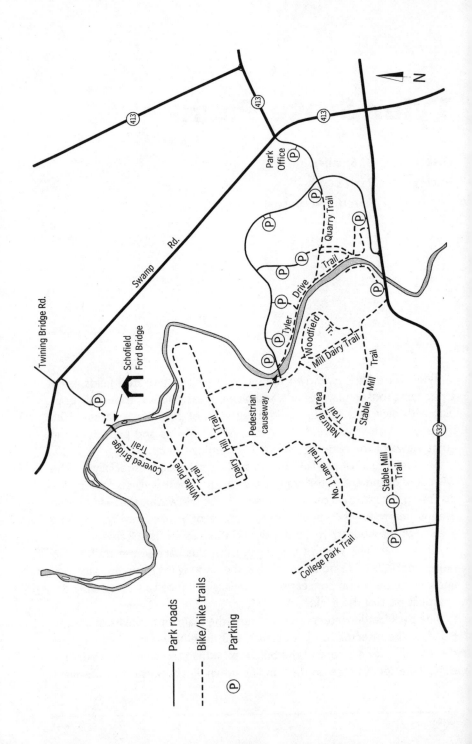

are also used by pedestrians. You wouldn't want to take a curve at high speed and find a pack of bird-watchers blocking the path ahead.

The park is also known for its equestrian trails, which are unpaved. Though the word is that they are great for all-terrain bicycling, official park policy limits bicyclists to the paved trails.

Check out the restored Schofield Ford Covered Bridge on the creek at the end of the Covered Bridge Trail. The bridge at this site was the longest covered bridge in Bucks County until it burned in 1991, but a group of volunteers have built a new bridge following the original design and using authentic materials and construction methods. The new bridge, which opened in 1997, can be reached via the paths from the main part of the park or by walking down an unpaved trail from a small parking area off Swamp Road.

Good to know:

Tyler State Park, 101 Swamp Rd., Newtown, (215) 968-2021 or 1-800-63-PARKS. Hiking, picnicking, playgrounds, ball fields, bike paths, equestrian trails, exercise trail, canoe rental, rest rooms.

For nearby food stops, see listings in Newtown on page 4.

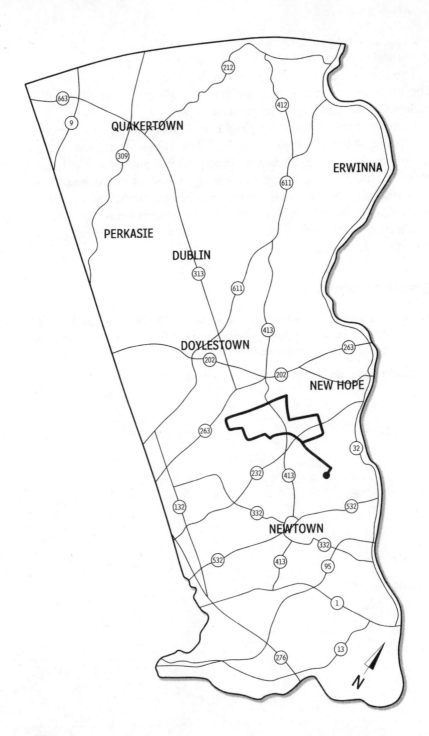

Wycombe

Distance: 23.0 miles
Rating: Medium
Start: Sol Feinstone Elementary School

This route takes you through the heart of an area that is located between the busy towns of Newtown and Doylestown yet seems miraculously to have been overlooked in the general rush to develop Bucks County.

The ride begins at the Sol Feinstone School or the adjacent Upper Makefield Township Building in Upper Makefield Township. To get there, take Eagle Road from Newtown, Pineville Road from Route 232, or Woodhill Road from Taylorsville Road. You'll find plenty of parking near these two buildings or by the soccer fields that lie between them. To reach the fields, turn at the municipal building and drive to the back of the property.

On Pineville Road, you'll pass a series of large and dignified old houses. Crossing Route 232 takes you into farmland and up to the intersection with Route 413 in Pineville. You can ride or walk your bike through a small parking lot and past the Pineville Tavern until you come even with Township Line Road on the other side of 413. Because there's no traffic light here, this is a somewhat tricky crossing. Once across, you'll continue on Township Line into Wycombe, the first of two tiny crossroads towns you'll pass through on this ride.

Wycombe is a town that feels old-fashioned and neighborly, with a post office, an old railroad station, a wholesaler of building and landscaping supplies, a restaurant called the Wycombe Inn, and not much else. Just past the railroad station, there's an old stone bridge over Mill Creek that partially collapsed after some flooding in 1996. A chain link fence was erected to block off the ruined part, and the bridge has been closed to motor vehicles while the powers that be decide what to do about it. The deliberations about the bridge are still going on, with one group advocating replacing it with a similar one-lane bridge and others pushing for something more modern. Meanwhile, it's an inconvenience to some motorists but a boon for bicyclists because it limits traffic along a couple of very scenic roads. The place where the bridge actually crosses the creek is a beautiful spot, well worth stopping to admire.

Past the bridge, you'll find yourself in rolling farm country. Smith Road dips down toward Robin Run and up again just below an earthen dam with a lake beyond. Mozart Road descends more steeply toward Neshaminy Creek, but if you want to actually see the water you'll have to take the detour to Dark Hollow Road described on the next page.

Lower Mountain Road brings you into Forest Grove, another little village along the lines of Wycombe. As you approach the town, there's a broad view of Buckingham Mountain straight ahead. On the other side of Route 413, you'll ride along the edge of the mountain before cutting back through farmland. Though Ridge Road itself is nearly flat, it provides a good view of Jericho Mountain to the south. Street Road and Buckmanville Road bring you back to Pineville Road for the return to the Sol Feinstone School.

Good to know:

Sandy's Country Store, Route 413, Pineville, (215) 598-3523. In the same building as the Pineville Post Office. This establishment specializes in gifts and foods from Scotland. You can get a cold drink and takeout food, as long as you're happy with a sausage roll or some other typically Scottish fare.

Variations:

Detour to Neshaminy Creek on Dark Hollow Rd. Dark Hollow crosses the creek on an iron bridge that is closed to cars. This side trip, which is both scenic and very peaceful, adds about 6.5 miles and a couple of robust climbs (on Wilkerson Rd. and Dark Hollow): When Smith Rd. ends at Swamp Rd., turn left instead of right. At the stop sign at the bottom of the hill, turn right onto Rushland Rd. Cross the creek and turn left onto Sacketts Ford Rd. Make the first right onto Wilkerson. When Wilkerson ends, turn right onto Walton Rd. There's a sweeping view here of distant hills. When Walton ends at a stop sign, turn left onto Rushland. Turn right onto Watson Rd. When Watson ends at a stop sign, turn right onto Almshouse Rd. Almshouse has no shoulder and carries a fair amount of traffic, but it is possible to ride the short stretch from Watson to Dark Hollow on the grass beside the road. Turn right onto Dark Hollow and ride across the bridge, which is closed to cars. Turn left onto Swamp to pick up the mapped route.

Shorten the route by starting in Wycombe. This cuts about 5.5 miles from the ride. There isn't really any on-street parking in town, but you could probably get away with taking a place in front of the post office on a Sunday or holiday when it's closed. Pick up the planned route at mile 5.2 in Wycombe, following the directions to mile 19.7, where Buckmanville Rd. ends at Pineville Rd. Turn right onto Pineville and follow the directions from the earlier part of the mapped route to return to Wycombe.

Start at Street Rd. and reverse the directions. Leave your car in the small clearing on Route 232 at Street Rd. Take Street Rd. north from 232. Go straight ahead on Ridge Rd. when Street Rd. turns to the right. Bear right onto New Rd. Turn right onto Holicong Rd. Turn left onto Lower Mountain Rd. Cross Route 413. Turn left onto Forest Grove Rd. Ride over the stone bridge into Wycombe. Continue straight on Township Line Rd. Cross Route 413 and walk your bike to the right in front of the Pineville Tavern to Pine La. Turn left onto Pine. Cross Route 232 and continue straight on Pineville Rd. Turn left onto Buckmanville Rd. Turn left onto Street Rd. and return to the parking area at Route 232. This version totals about 13.2 miles.

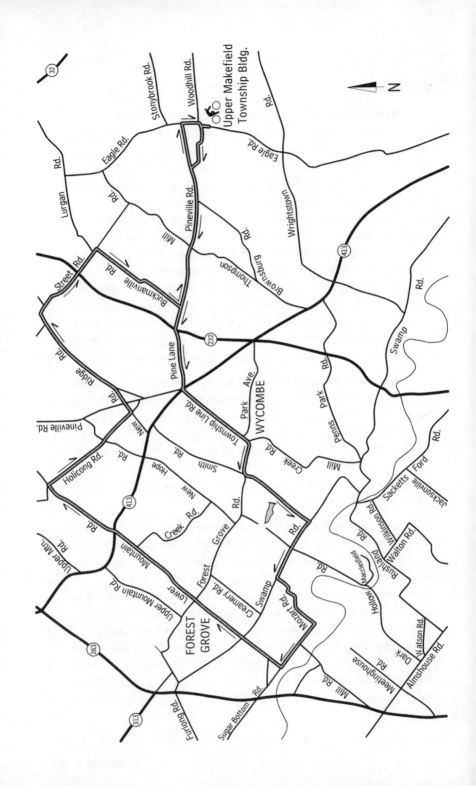

Directions:

0.0 From the Township Building driveway, turn **right** onto Eagle Rd.

0.3 When Eagle appears to end at a stop sign, turn **left** onto Woodhill Rd.

1.0 When Woodhill ends at a stop sign, turn **left** onto Pineville Rd.

3.2 At a stop sign, cross Route 232 (Windy Bush Rd.) and continue **straight** on Pine La.

3.9 At the stop sign at Route 413, turn **right** and walk your bike to the Pineville Tavern. Carefully cross Route 413 to Township Line Rd.

4.0 Continue **straight** ahead on Township Line.

5.2 At the railroad tracks, bear **right** onto Forest Grove Rd. Cross the bridge over Mill Creek and continue on Forest Grove.

5.6 Turn **left** onto Smith Rd.

6.7 Turn **right** onto Swamp Rd.

7.6 Turn **left** onto Mozart Rd. (It becomes Sugar Bottom Rd.)

9.2 Turn **right** onto Lower Mountain Rd.

12.3 At a stop sign, carefully cross Route 413 and continue **straight** on Lower Mountain.

13.5 At a stop sign, turn **right** onto Holicong Rd.

15.0 Turn **left** onto New Rd.

15.4 Turn **left** onto Ridge Rd. (It becomes Street Rd.)

17.8 Cross Route 232 and continue **straight** ahead on Street.

18.2 Turn **right** onto Buckmanville Rd.

19.7 When Buckmanville ends at a stop sign, turn **left** onto Pineville Rd.

22.2 When Pineville ends at a stop sign, turn **right** onto Eagle.

22.5 Follow Eagle as it bends to the right, then bear **left** to stay on Eagle when Woodhill goes **straight** ahead.

23.0 Turn **left** to return to the parking area.

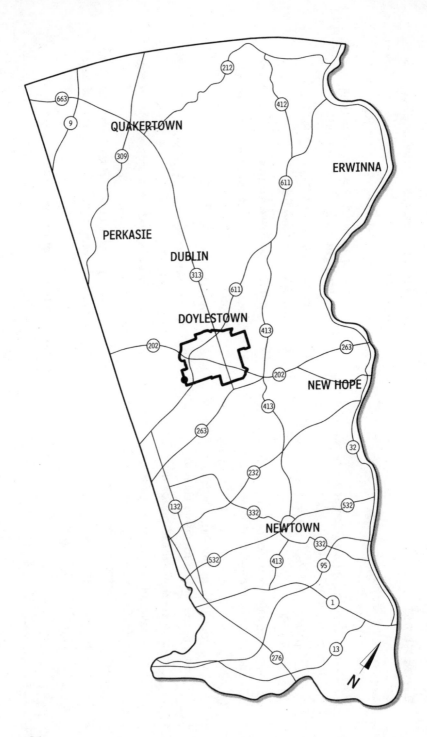

Doylestown

Distance: 16.3 miles
Rating: Medium
Start: Central Park

This ride loops in a large circle around Doylestown, which is the biggest town in the central part of Bucks County and the seat of county government. It's a place that is in the process of being reborn, with a new art museum housed in a former prison, a restored vintage movie theater specializing in films that are a cut above most of the dozen playing at your local multiplex, and a good selection of restaurants offering varying cuisines and price levels. However, this ride stays away from the center of town, which despite its many charms is clogged with too much traffic for pleasant bicycle touring except at off times, such as very early on a weekend morning.

Cycling around Doylestown, you'll pass quite a few of the old stone houses that are so characteristic of this region, as well as several of the brand new developments that have become the new standard for housing here. These developments might not do much for the scenery, but they do provide a way for cyclists to avoid some of the busier roads.

The ride begins at Central Park, a name that always makes me chuckle although it is actually quite a nice facility, with basketball and tennis courts, soccer fields, and plenty of parking. The easiest way to find it is to pick up Lower State Road in Doylestown (it's the extension of West Court Street) and turn left onto Wells Road. The centerpiece of the park is an elaborately constructed children's play area called Kids' Castle. A paved path runs around this area, but it's mostly too steep for beginning cyclists and too short to be of much interest to anyone else.

From the park you'll ride north on Wells Road, turning into a development at Vale View Drive in order to avoid riding on New Britain Road. On the other side of New Britain, the route runs through Delaware Valley College in order to avoid crossing Route 202 (East Butler Avenue) at an intersection without a traffic signal. Inside the college grounds, signs marked "Exit to 202" direct traffic toward the left and through the school's main parking areas. Bicyclists can ignore the signs and continue straight ahead using roads that are closed to cars. Both ways bring you to the light at the main campus entrance from Route 202, where you'll cross 202 and continue through an older residential neighborhood on Iron Hill Road.

From there, the ride is straightforward to Old Dublin Pike, passing houses and farms. You'll cross Route 313 (Swamp Road) at a traffic signal and continue on to North Easton Road. This is a four-lane road and there's no traffic signal here, so caution is in order, but you shouldn't have to wait long for a chance to get across.

On the other side of North Easton the countryside turns rural again, although development is claiming large slices of this area, too. You'll find a nice little village near the intersection of Old Easton Road and Stony

Lane and some pretty old houses along Mill Road just before Route 202. You'll need to pay attention here, because this crossing also takes place at an intersection without a traffic signal.

Just after Route 202, when Mill Road goes off to the left, the ride route turns onto Furlong Road and from there to Spring Valley Road. Most of this last part of the ride is pleasant but unexceptional. You'll want to take special care once again when Spring Valley Road crosses back over Swamp Road at an intersection without a traffic signal.

Although there's nothing commercial directly on this route, there are plenty of places to stop for refreshments in Doylestown before or after the ride, including most of the usual fast-food brands.

Good to know:

Bagel Barrel, 60 W. State St., Doylestown, (215) 348-8280. Bagels, etc., in the center of town.

Central Park, 425 Wells Rd., Doylestown, (215) 348-9915. Ball fields, basketball and tennis courts, playground, rest rooms.

County Theatre, 20 E. State St., Doylestown, (215) 348-3456. An old movie house, recently restored, specializing in quality films that don't always get the attention they deserve in the big theaters.

Fonthill Museum, E. Court St. at the intersection with East St., Doylestown, (215) 348-9461. Tile-encrusted, reinforced-concrete building that was home to the eccentric Henry Chapman Mercer, now a county museum. Chapman's tileworks, still in operation, are also located on the property. Admission charged.

James A. Michener Art Museum, 128 S. Pine St., Doylestown, (215) 340-9800. Located in a restored 19th-century prison, with its own cappuccino bar, featuring Bucks County artists. Admission charged.

Peacock Cafe, 54 E. State St., Doylestown, (215) 348-8083. A sit-down place for breakfast, lunch, or ice cream, but put together with a lot more atmosphere than the typical luncheonette.

Sandwich Connection, 3611 Old Easton Rd., Doylestown, (215) 340-9104. Just a deli, but they make particularly good sandwiches.

7-Eleven Food Store, 495 East St., Doylestown, (215) 348-1710. The usual.

Wawa Food Market, 339 S. Main St., Doylestown, (215) 345-4160. Likewise, if you've seen one, you've seen 'em all.

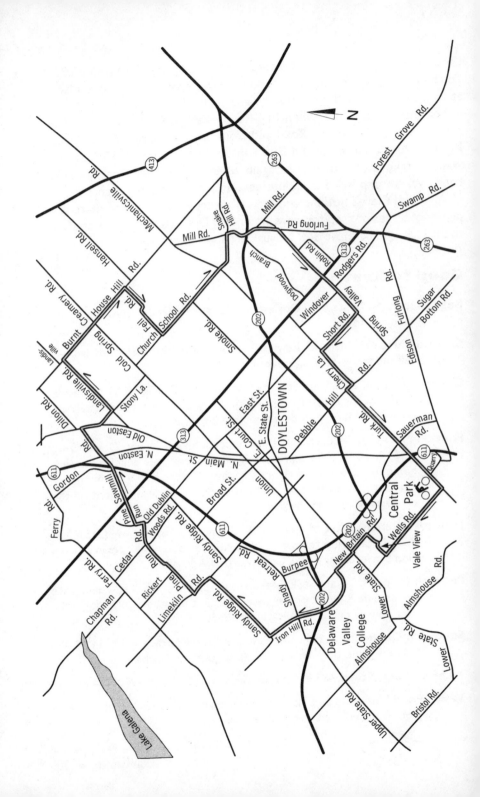

Directions:

0.0 Turn **right** from Central Park onto Wells Rd.

0.5 Turn **right** into the development at Vale View Dr.

0.6 When Vale View ends at a stop sign, turn **left** onto Sunset View Dr.

0.8 When Sunset View ends at a stop sign, turn **left** onto New Britain Rd.

1.1 At the stop sign at Lower State Rd., go **left then right** to continue on New Britain Rd.

1.3 Turn **left** into Delaware Valley College. Ride straight through the college to the main entrance on the other side. (You can ignore the signs marked "Exit to 202" and stay on roads that are closed to car traffic.)

2.1 At the traffic light, cross Route 202 (E. Butler Ave.) and continue **straight** ahead on Iron Hill Rd.

2.8 When Iron Hill ends at a stop sign, turn **right** onto Sandy Ridge Rd.

3.8 When Sandy Ridge ends at a stop sign, turn **left** onto Limekiln Rd.

4.0 Turn **right** onto Pine Run Rd.

5.1 When Pine Run ends at a stop sign, turn **left** onto Old Dublin Pk.

5.2 At the end of the stone bridge, turn **right** onto Pine Run Rd.

5.5 At the traffic signal, cross Route 313 (Swamp Rd.) and continue **straight** ahead on Sawmill Rd.

6.1 At the stop sign, cross N. Easton Rd. carefully (it's a four-lane road here) and continue **straight** ahead on Sawmill.

6.6 When Sawmill ends at a stop sign, turn **right** onto Old Easton Rd.

6.8 Bear **left** onto Stony La.

7.0 When Stony appears to end at a stop sign, turn **left** onto Landisville Rd.

7.8 When Landisville appears to end at a stop sign, turn **right** onto Burnt House Hill Rd.

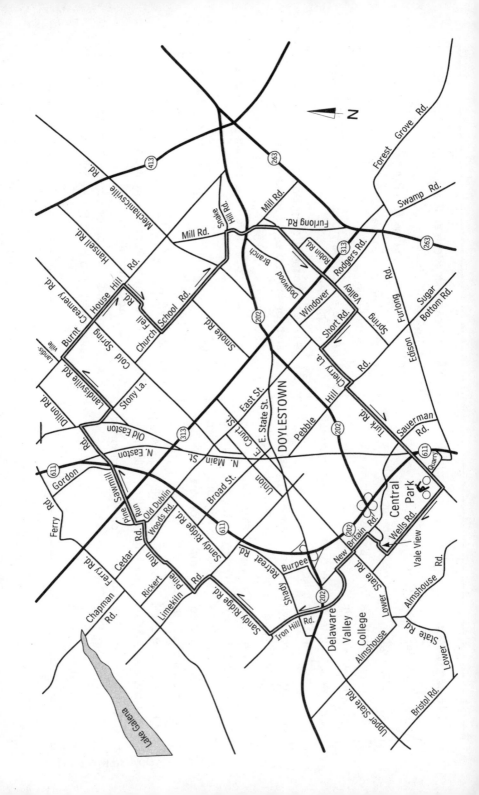

8.9 At the top of the hill, turn **right** onto Fell Rd.

9.7 When Fell ends at a stop sign, turn **left** onto Church School Rd.

10.7 At a stop sign, cross Mechanicsville Rd. and continue **straight** ahead on Church School.

11.1 At the stop sign, turn **right** onto Mill Rd.

11.4 At the stop sign, cross Route 202 carefully and continue **straight** ahead on Mill.

11.5 When Mill goes off to the left, bear **right** onto Furlong Rd.

11.8 Turn **right** onto Spring Valley Rd.

12.5 At the stop sign, cross Route 313 (Swamp) carefully and continue **straight** ahead on Spring Valley.

13.1 Turn **right** onto Short Rd.

13.7 When Short ends at a stop sign, turn **left** onto Cherry La.

14.3 At the stop sign, turn **right** onto Pebble Hill Rd.

14.3 Make the next **left** onto Turk Rd.

16.0 Turn **right** onto Wells Rd.

16.3 Turn **right** into Central Park.

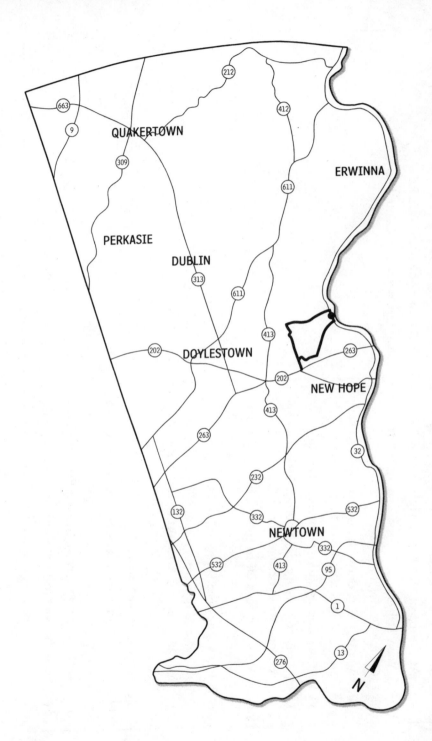

Peddler's Village

Distance: 12.0 miles
Rating: Medium
Start: Lumberville

This ride has three of the ingredients that charm visitors to Bucks County: A quaint little town on the Delaware River, miles of scenic countryside, and shopping in a place where both the stores and the merchandise break the mold of what's available in every mall in America.

In this case the town is Lumberville, a pretty half-mile strip of old houses perched above the river about six miles north of New Hope. There's a pedestrian bridge that stretches out above the river to New Jersey, and there are picnic tables next to the Delaware Canal just north of the bridge. You can cross over to the canal towpath near these tables and ride or walk along the river. There isn't much by way of commerce in Lumberville, although the Lumberville Store does offer refreshments and an eclectic array of merchandise.

Peddler's Village is a different story, of course. The village is located at the intersection of Routes 202 and 263 in Lahaska; it's easy to find, especially on weekends, when it tends to become the center of the biggest traffic jam in the central Bucks area. It's laid out to resemble an old-fashioned town that is always carefully landscaped and well-supplied with benches where you can rest and enjoy looking at the flowers and the other shoppers. More than seventy shops sell everything from quilts to doll houses to kitchen gadgets, and there are eleven different places to eat and drink. (The five most casual are listed here; Peddler's Village is a tourist destination, so most everyone is informally dressed, but you might not feel right in some of the nicer restaurants in sweaty cycling clothes.)

Between Lumberville and Peddler's Village lies a selection of Bucks County countryside that ranges from rolling farmland to woods and streams. You can park at either end of the ride, although if you choose to start in Lumberville it's probably best to leave your car at New Jersey's Bull's Island Recreation Area, on the other side of the pedestrian bridge over the Delaware River. You can reach it by crossing the river at Stockton and driving north on Route 29 in New Jersey.

From Lumberville, the ride uses scenic Fleecydale Road for the climb up from the river. It's marked as closed to all but local traffic because it narrows to one lane in some places, but it's easily passable by bicycle. You'll be going uphill here, but it's a gradual climb from Lumberville to the town of Carversville, where the Carversville General Store offers another option for refreshments.

From Lumberville it's about six and a half miles to Peddler's Village, where you can leave your bike for a while and explore by foot. When you're ready to return, you'll start by tackling the biggest hill on the ride, the climb from Street Road up Honey Hollow Road to Hidden Valley Drive. On Greenhill Road, you can visit the biggest farmer's market in the area if you happen to be riding by on a Tuesday or Saturday morning. Rice's Market has rows and rows of tables displaying a wide variety of merchandise and there are several different places to get refreshments, but bicyclists should be warned that traffic on nearby roads goes up dramatically when the market is open.

Good to know:

Animal Crackers, Peddler's Village, (215) 794-4000. The Peddler's Village version of fast food, with pizza, hot dogs, croissant sandwiches, etc.

Auntie Em's Cookie Shop, Peddler's Village, (215) 794-4000. Ice cream and homemade cookies.

Bull's Island Recreation Area, 2185 Daniel Bray Hwy. (Route 29), Stockton, N.J., (609) 397-2949. On the Delaware three miles north of the center of Stockton, with access to the canal paths on both sides of the river, picnicking, rest rooms, camping. Pedestrian bridge to Lumberville in Pennsylvania.

The gazebo, a shaded place to rest at Peddler's Village

Carversville General Store, Aquetong and Fleecydale rds., Carversville, (215) 297-5353. A real old-fashioned country store, home to the Carversville Post Office, with sandwiches and cold drinks available.

House of Coffee, Peddler's Village, (215) 794-794-8220. Coffee by the cup or by the pound.

Lumberville Store & Gallery, 3744 River Rd., Lumberville, (215) 297-5388. Food to go, arts and crafts, books, and bicycle rentals. A very nice place to begin your ride or enjoy a halfway break.

Rice's Sale and Country Market, 6326 Greenhill Rd., Solebury Township, (215) 297-5993. A farm where the fields have been turned into parking areas and selling space for vendors of merchandise from jewelry to sportswear to spices; the biggest flea market around. Open Tuesday and Saturday A.M.

Village Cafe, Peddler's Village, (215) 794-5980. An informal place to enjoy a sandwich or specialty quiche.

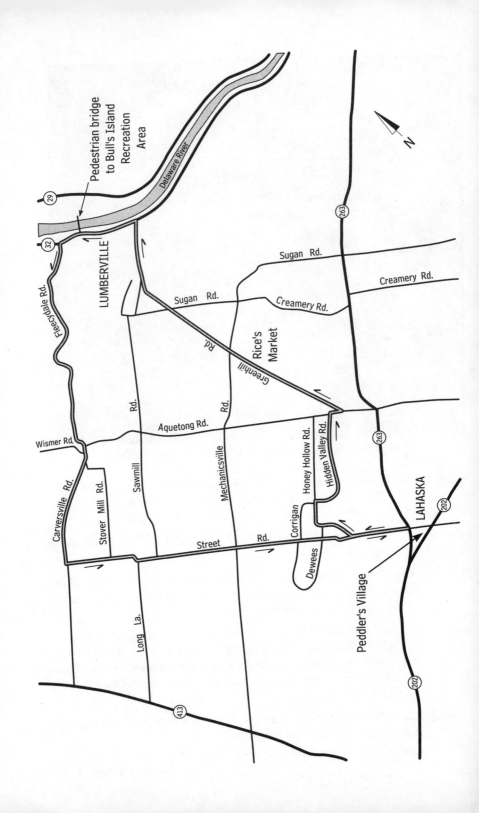

Directions:

0.0 From the pedestrian bridge in Lumberville, ride north on Route 32 (River Rd.).

0.2 At the end of the one-lane bridge, turn **left** onto Fleecydale Rd.

2.3 At the stop sign in Carversville, turn **right** onto Carversville Rd.

2.4 When the road forks, bear **right** to stay on Carversville.

3.4 Turn **left** onto Street Rd.

4.1 When Long La. goes off ahead, turn **left** to continue on Street Rd.

5.0 Cross Mechanicsville and continue **straight** ahead on Street.

6.7 When you reach the stop sign at Route 263, you'll see Peddler's Village ahead and to your right. To return to Lumberville, turn around here and head back on Street Rd.

7.2 Turn **right** onto Honey Hollow Rd.

7.6 Turn **right** onto Hidden Valley Dr.

8.5 When Hidden Valley ends at a stop sign, turn **right** onto Aquetong Rd.

8.6 At the stop sign, turn **left** onto Greenhill Rd.

9.2 Pass Rice's Market.

9.8 At the stop sign, cross Mechanicsville Rd. and continue **straight** ahead on Greenhill.

11.5 At the stop sign, turn **left** onto Route 32. (Be careful; traffic here goes fast.)

12.0 Return to Lumberville.

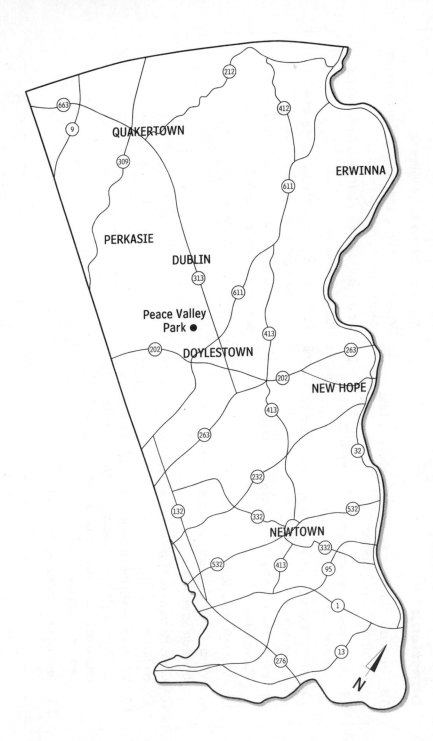

Peace Valley Park

Distance: 6.3 miles

Rating: Easy

Paved bike path

   The last time I rode at Peace Valley was a Sunday afternoon in late fall when my family decided we should go for a ride together. I've never been a tremendous fan of park bike paths, preferring something a little more interesting, and frankly, I wasn't expecting much, but before long I was wondering if there were anyplace more beautiful in all of Bucks County. The water was incredibly blue, we had a sweeping view of red and yellow trees on the far side of Lake Galena, and the path itself was surprisingly uncrowded.

   The actual paved paths, which are shared with pedestrians and skaters, extend only part way around the lake. To go all the way around, cyclists must also use Creek Road, which has very little traffic, and New Galena Road, which has a little more. The complete loop totals 6.3 miles.

   The most important thing to remember if you're planning to ride all the way around the lake is to make the circuit in a clockwise direction. The paths in the park are gently rolling, and the only serious climb you'll encounter if you ride clockwise is on New Galena Road between the park entrance and Chapman Road, but it's a long, relatively gradual rise. However, Chapman from New Galena to the nature center is rather steep, and not many cyclists can make it from the nature center to the

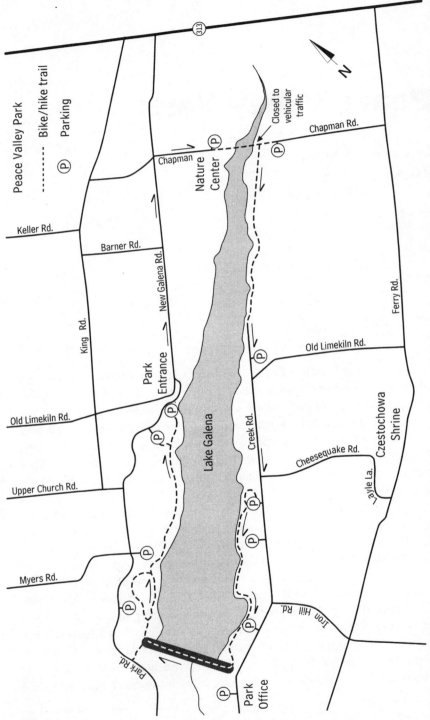

Peace Valley Park

- - - - - Bike/hike trail
Ⓟ Parking

313

N

Keller Rd.

Barner Rd.

New Galena Rd.

King Rd.

Park Entrance

Old Limekiln Rd.

Upper Church Rd.

Myers Rd.

Park Rd.

Lake Galena

Creek Rd.

Chapman

Nature Center

Chapman Rd.

Closed to vehicular traffic

Ferry Rd.

Old Limekiln Rd.

Cheesequake Rd.

Czestochowa Shrine

Gayle La.

Iron Hill Rd.

Park Office

top of the hill without getting off to walk. Riders looking for something really easy would do best to stick to the area near the dam at the western end of the park.

To get to Peace Valley Park, take Route 313 west from Doylestown and turn left onto New Galena Road. Go about two miles down New Galena and you'll come to a big park entrance. In addition to bike paths, the park has picnic tables, fishing piers, a boat launch ramp, and boat rentals, as well as a nature center with organized programs and trails. The large grassy areas that sweep down toward the water are popular with sunbathers in warmer weather. These facilities are served by a series of parking lots around the lake. Because its many attractions make this park extremely popular with families, early morning and late afternoon are probably the best times to find things relatively uncrowded.

You can't buy refreshments in the park itself, but all the pleasures of Doylestown lie just a few miles away on Route 313. See listings on page 39 for details.

Good to know:

Peace Valley Park, 230 Creek Rd., New Britain, (215) 822-8608. Picnicking, boating, fishing, boat rental, nature trails and special programs at Peace Valley Nature Center.

Roman Delight, Route 313, Fountainville, 215-348-2222. Pizza place not too far from the park, at the intersection of Route 313 and Ferry Rd.

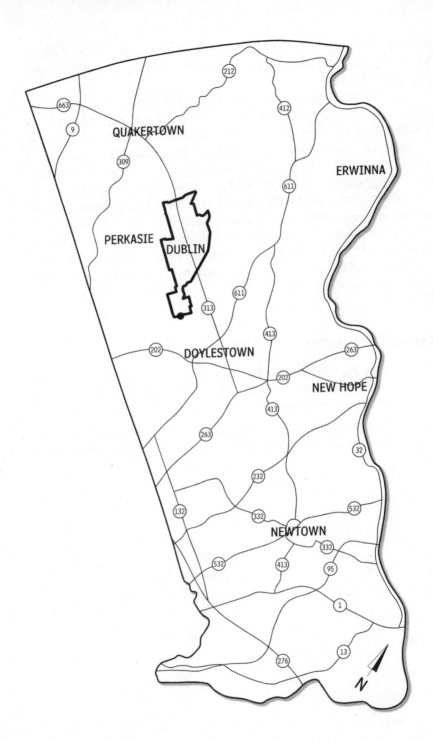

The lakes

Distance:	**22.6 miles**
Rating:	**Difficult**
Start:	**Nockamixon State Park**
	or Peace Valley Park

Northwest of Doylestown there are two magnificent artificial lakes that would have to rank high on any list of Bucks County's scenic pleasures. Lake Galena and Lake Nockamixon both have parks with bike paths for those who wish to enjoy the landscape by way of some relatively tame riding, but this route between the two lakes offers maximum enjoyment of the view and covers more challenging terrain.

The direct route between the lakes would take you about seven and a half miles down Route 313. This route stays on the smaller roads that wander through the farmland on either side of that busy thoroughfare, and it takes some serious riding to climb from the lakes up into that middle ground.

You can begin this ride at either lake, although the directions that follow describe the route starting at the entrance to Peace Valley Park on New Galena Road. (See page 51 for more about Peace Valley.) There's a good hill going up Barner Road, but things improve somewhat after that. You'll be riding mostly through rolling farmland in an area that is really quite rural until you come into the borough of Dublin on Middle Road. Be careful at the stop sign at Maple Avenue and at the traffic light where you cross Route 313. After that, you'll be back in farmland again as ou ride along Elephant Rd. (This unusual name is derived from the tiny town called Elephant at the intersection of Elephant and Ridge roads. The town was named after a hotel called the Elephant, which is still there, but I don't know where the name of the hotel came from.)

At the Three-Mile Run Boat Access Area on the south shore of Lake Nockamixon, you'll find rest rooms and a good view of the lake (as well as plenty of parking for those who choose to start the ride at this end; see page 85 for more information about this park). Three-Mile Run Road is wooded and fairly flat, with a panoramic vista of a distant ridge on the west side of Route 313. The next big challenge comes at the turn onto Schwenk Mill Road, which is steeply uphill to start and very steeply downhill and winding after it crosses Route 563 (Ridge Road). This section has some of the best scenery on the ride, but it also presents the most difficult riding. You can't let yourself pick up too much speed on the downhill, either, because the stop sign at Fifth Street comes soon after the bottom of the hill.

After that, you'll be riding mostly through farmland again until the approach to Lake Galena on Upper Church Road. The last part of the ride takes you through Peace Valley Park and past some excellent views of Lake Galena.

You'll pass a couple of farm stands on this ride: the Tabora Farm Market, just to your left on Upper Stump Road as you cross it on Upper Church Road, and the Penn View Dairy Store, on Broad Street as you cross it on Middle Road. Other than that, your best bets for refreshments are a little off the mapped route on Route 313 in Dublin. This is a busy road and not recommended for cycling, but the Dairy Queen and Luberto's Pizza are both a short walk on the sidewalk to the left (west) from the light at Route 313.

Good to know:

Dairy Queen, 106 N. Main St., Dublin. A classic in the heart of Dublin; you'll see it half a block to the left when you hit the traffic light at Maple and Route 313.

Luberto's Brick Oven Pizza, 169 N. Main St., Dublin, (215) 249-0688. A little past Dairy Queen on Route 313.

Nockamixon State Park, 1542 Mountain View Dr., Quakertown, (215) 529-7300 or 1-800-63-PARKS. Boating, boat rentals, fishing, picnicking, bike path, equestrian trails, rest rooms. Swimming pool; admission charged.

Variations:

Use Blue School Rd. to shorten the ride. You can cut across Blue School Rd. to make a shorter ride from either direction. This creates a loop of about 16 miles starting from Lake Galena or about 12 miles starting from Lake Nockamixon. If you take this variation from Lake Galena, you'll still have some hills to climb but you'll skip the downhill on Schwenk Mill Rd., which is probably the most difficult stretch of road on the ride.

Start in Dublin for a 12-mile ride without huge hills. Park at the borough public recreation area on Middle Rd. about a half mile west of the traffic light at Route 313. Turn right onto Middle Road and follow the directions to the intersection of Elephant Rd. and Blue School Rd. Turn left on Blue School and take it to Blooming Glen Rd. Turn left on Blooming Glen and follow the directions until Welcome House Rd. ends at Broad St. Turn left on Broad and take it back to Middle Rd. Turn left on Middle and follow it back to the recreation area.

Go straight across Elephant Rd. There's a tough climb on Elephant Rd. just after Sweetbriar Rd., but that isn't why the planned route turns off onto Sweetbriar. The problem with approaching Lake Nockamixon on Elephant Rd. is that you'll hit a very sharp turn to the left at the bottom of a steep hill. If this sounds like fun, continue straight ahead on Elephant at mile 9.8, crossing Ridge at the stop sign. Cross Old Bethlehem Rd. at the stop sign at the bottom of the hill and continue on the planned route around the bend and past the boat access on Three-Mile Run Rd. This cuts about a mile from the ride.

Penn View Farm, 1433 Broad St., Perkasie, (215) 249-9128. At the intersection with Middle Rd.

Peace Valley Park, 230 Creek Rd., New Britain, (215) 822-8608. Picnicking, boating, fishing, boat rental, nature trails and special programs at Peace Valley Nature Center.

Tabora Farm & Orchard, 1104 Upper Stump Rd., Chalfont, (215) 249-3016. Just off Upper Church Rd.

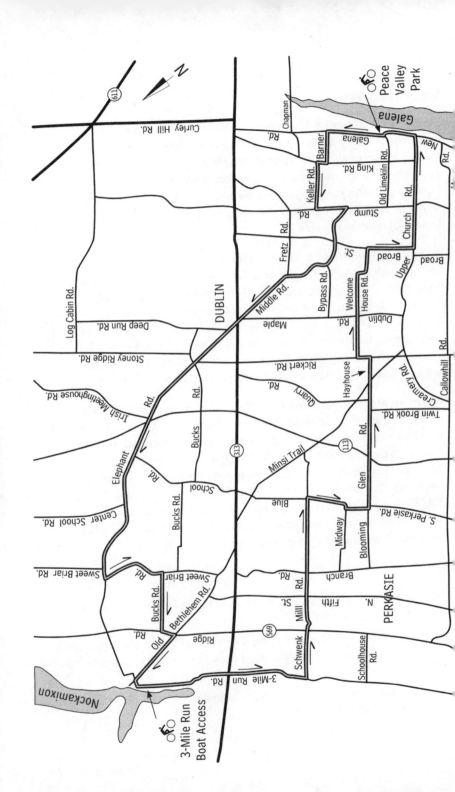

Directions:

0.0 At the stop sign at the entrance to Peace Valley Park, turn **right** onto New Galena Rd.

0.6 Turn **left** onto Barner Rd.

1.0 When Barner ends at a stop sign, turn **right** onto King Rd.

1.1 Turn **left** onto Keller Rd. (Watch out crossing the metal grate at the bottom of the hill on Keller.)

1.7 When Keller ends at a stop sign, turn **left** onto Stump Rd.

2.1 Turn **right** onto Middle Rd.

2.6 At the stop sign at Broad St., go **straight** ahead to continue on Middle.

3.0 When Bypass Rd. goes off to the left, bear **right** to continue on Middle.

4.3 When Middle ends at a stop sign, turn **right** onto Maple.

4.3 At the traffic signal, cross Route 313 and continue **straight** ahead on Elephant Rd.

6.1 At a stop sign, cross Route 113 (Bedminster Rd.) and continue **straight** ahead on Elephant.

8.3 Turn **left** onto Sweet Briar Rd.

9.1 Turn **right** onto Bucks Rd.

9.9 When Bucks ends at a stop sign, turn **left** onto Ridge Rd.

10.1 Turn **right** onto Old Bethlehem Rd.

10.9 At a stop sign, turn **left** onto Elephant. (It bends to the left and becomes Three-Mile Run Rd.)

11.2 Pass the Three-Mile Run Boat Access Area at Nockamixon State Park.

12.1 At the stop sign, carefully cross Route 313 and continue **straight** ahead on Three-Mile Run.

13.2 Turn **left** onto Schwenk Mill Rd.

13.8 At the stop sign, cross Route 563 (Ridge Rd.) and continue **straight** ahead on Schwenk Mill. **Be very careful:** The first part of Schwenk Mill south of Ridge is extremely steep and winding, and you'll come to a stop sign not long after the hill levels out.

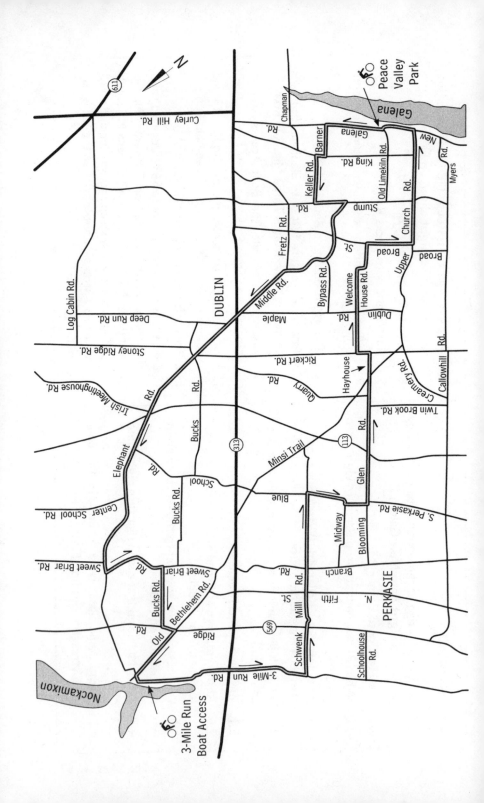

14.3 At the stop sign, cross Fifth St. and continue **straight** ahead on Schwenk Mill.

15.6 At the stop sign, turn **right** onto Blue School Rd.

16.1 When Midway Rd. goes straight ahead, turn **left** to continue on Blue School.

16.4 When Blue School ends at a stop sign, turn **left** onto Blooming Glen Rd.

18.1 At a stop sign, cross Minsi Trail and continue **straight** ahead on Hayhouse Rd.

18.4 When Hayhouse ends at a stop sign, turn **left** onto Rickert Rd.

18.5 Turn **right** onto Welcome House Rd.

20.1 When Welcome House ends at a stop sign, turn **right** onto Broad St.

20.7 When Broad appears to end at a stop sign, turn **left** onto Upper Church Rd.

21.2 At the stop sign, cross Upper Stump Rd. and continue **straight** ahead on Upper Church. Be careful: From here, Upper Church goes very steeply downhill.

21.8 At the stop sign, cross King and continue **straight** ahead.

21.9 When Upper Church ends, turn **left** onto New Galena.

22.6 Return to the park entrance.

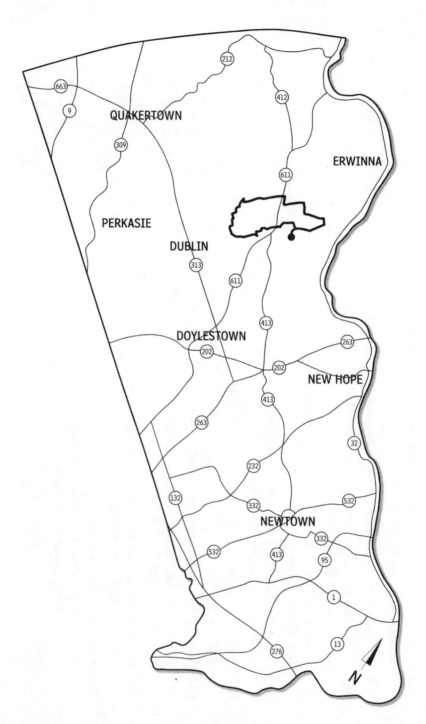

Bedminster & Tinicum

Distance: 18.2 miles
Rating: Difficult
Start: Stover-Myers Mill

This ride is perfect for lovers of natural scenery because it rolls along past some extremely pretty countryside—and not much else. To be perfectly fair, the center of the town of Bedminster can found at the intersection of Route 113 and Kellers Church Road. It has a post office and a municipal building as well as a group of houses, but unless you have an urgent need for stamps, there isn't much reason to stop there.

For the most part, the route takes you through woods and rolling farmland in an area where there are enough hills to provide lovely panoramic views of barns, silos and green fields. Because of the number of hills and the fact that a few are rather steep—and in the case of Oak Grove Road toward the end of the route, also fairly rough—I've put the ride in the "difficult" category. I consider it to be only a little more challenging than some of the medium rides in this book, however.

The route begins at the parking lot for the Stover-Myers Mill, which is part of the Bucks County park system. To get there from Route 413, turn onto Dark Hollow Road. (Dark Hollow has a four-way stop and it's the last intersection before 413 joins Route 611.) Follow Dark Hollow to the bottom of the hill, and the parking area will be on your right.

Tohickon Creek and Covered Bridge Road run side by side

You'll begin by riding on Dark Hollow Road along Tohickon Creek, with a nice view of the creek from a bridge that crosses it just after the mill. After that, you'll leave Tohickon Creek behind and pick up Tinicum Creek, which flows along next to Hollow Horn and Red Hill roads as they bring you toward Route 611.

You'll cross 611 at an intersection without a traffic signal, but it shouldn't be difficult to get over. On the other side, Farm School Road crosses an unusual metal bridge over Tohickon Creek, then takes you mostly through rolling farmland until it ends at Kellers Church Road. The turn onto Kellers Church Road will bring you up a short hill, but your efforts here will be rewarded with an excellent view of the town of Bedminster once you turn onto Fretz Valley Road. This part of the ride seems to alternate between hills and valleys; you'll travel through a very pretty little valley along Deep Run just before you return to Route 611, which you'll cross again at an intersection without a traffic signal.

The last part of the ride uses Gruver Road instead of Randts Mill Road because Randts Mill is unpaved and tends to be a little swampy when the weather is wet, and quite uneven when it's dry. (In the mud season, I have come perilously close to being absolutely stuck on this road in a car.)

Variations:

Ride along Covered Bridge Rd. to the Cabin Run Covered Bridge. This road carries very little traffic and is easy riding as it follows Tohickon Creek about a half mile from the Stover-Myers Mill parking area to the covered bridge over Cabin Run. It's only a short detour, and it's very pretty.

Ride along Meadow La. beside Deep Run. Just before the left turn from Hill Rd. onto Irish Meetinghouse Rd. at mile 12.4 in the planned route, Meadow La. goes off to the left. It rolls along beside Deep Run through a secluded valley for about three-quarters of a mile before ending at Kellers Church Rd., which is steeply uphill in either direction at this point. This makes a beautiful little detour if you're in the mood to check it out.

Shorten the ride slightly by riding down Kellers Church Rd. At mile 10.9 in the directions, turn left from Farm School Rd. onto Kellers Church Rd. and follow it to rejoin the planned route again at Quarry Rd. at mile 12.3 This detour knocks about two and a half miles off the total, with nothing lost but scenery.

Shorten the ride even more by riding across Oak Grove Rd. You can turn left instead of right onto Oak Grove Rd. at mile 6.1 in the directions and ride to Gruver Rd. Make left onto Gruver and pick up the directions again at mile 16.6. This trims the ride to about nine miles total and eliminates the most serious hills. Unfortunately, it also misses a lot of the prettiest scenery.

There are picnic tables and rest rooms at the mill, but if you want to stop and relax here at the end of the ride you'd best bring your refreshments from somewhere else.

Good to know:

Stover-Myers Mill, Dark Hollow Rd., one mile east of Pipersville, (215) 757-0571 (Bucks County Parks Dept.). Restored mill on Tohickon Creek, built around 1800. Picnicking, rest rooms.

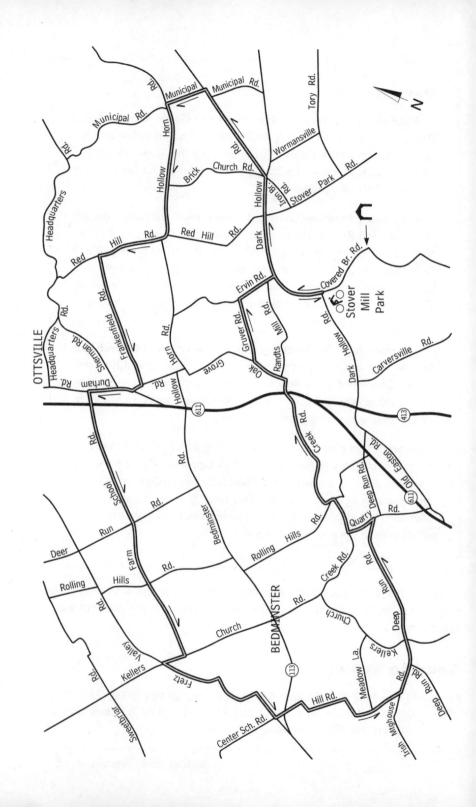

Directions:

0.0 From the parking lot for the Stover-Myers Mill, turn **left** onto Covered Bridge Rd. and ride toward the mill. Go straight at the stop sign onto Dark Hollow Rd.

1.4 Just after Christ Lutheran Church, bear **left** to stay on Dark Hollow Rd. (The hard left is Brick Church Rd.)

2.4 Turn **left** onto Municipal Rd.

2.8 When the road ends at a stop sign, turn **left** onto Hollow Horn Rd.

4.1 When Hollow Horn goes off to the left, go **straight** ahead onto Red Hill Rd.

4.7 Turn **left** onto Frankenfield Rd.

6.1 When Frankenfield ends at a stop sign, turn **right** onto Oak Grove Rd.

6.1 Make the first **right** onto Durham Rd.

6.6 Turn **left** onto Farm School Rd.

6.8 At the stop sign, cross Route 611 carefully and continue **straight** ahead on Farm School.

9.3 When Farm School ends at a stop sign, turn **right** onto Kellers Church Rd.

9.6 Turn **left** onto Fretz Valley Rd.

10.8 Just after the Bedminster Elementary School, turn **left** onto Center School Rd.

11.0 At the stop sign, cross Route 113 (Bedminster Rd.) and continue **straight** ahead on Hill Rd.

12.4 When Hill ends at a stop sign, turn **left** onto Irish Meetinghouse Rd.

12.7 At the stop sign where Deep Run Rd. comes in from the right, continue **straight** ahead on Deep Run.

14.1 Make a hard **left** onto Quarry Rd.

14.4 When Quarry ends at a stop sign, turn **right** onto Creek Rd.

14.8 At a stop sign, turn **left** onto Rolling Hills Rd.

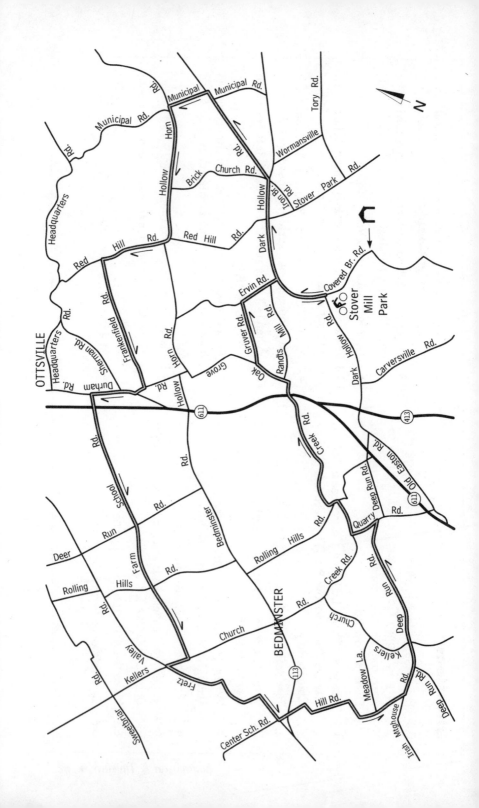

14.7 When Rolling Hills goes off to the left, stay to the **right** to continue on Creek Rd.

16.1 At a stop sign, cross Route 611 carefully and continue **straight** ahead on Oak Grove Rd.

16.6 Turn **right** onto Gruver Rd.

17.2 When Gruver ends at a stop, turn **right** onto Ervin Rd.

17.6 When Ervin ends at a stop, turn **right** onto Dark Hollow.

18.2 Return to the parking lot at Stover-Myers Mill.

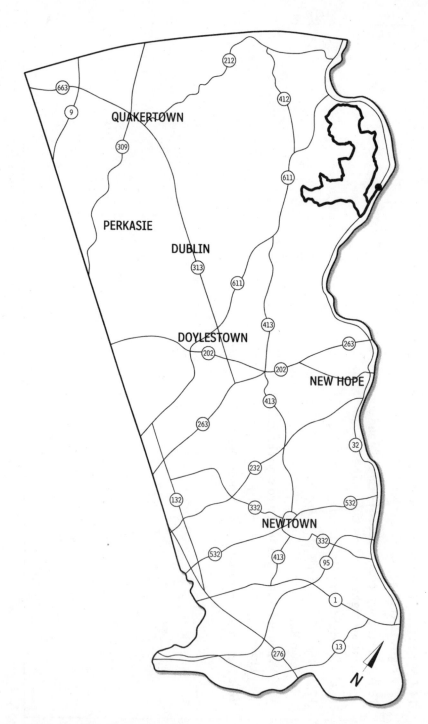

The northeast

Distance: 28.1 miles
Rating: Difficult
Start: Tinicum Park

There's a hump along the northeast edge of Bucks County where the land seems to protrude both upward and outward, raising a high plateau and pushing toward New Jersey, forcing the Delaware River to swing wide around it. This outcropping of land is surrounded on all sides by steep hills, and these hills are what makes this ride challenging.

The route begins at Tinicum Park on Route 32 (River Road) in Erwinna, site of a well-known annual arts festival as well as a Fourth of July pops concert that draws thousands to hear a local orchestra while picnicking on a wide grassy lawn. The park is about three-quarters of a mile south of the bridge over the Delaware to Frenchtown, N.J. You'll find the usual outdoor tables and restrooms here, and there's also an area where camping is permitted.

After a short ride on River Road, the route turns westward, taking you through the covered bridge in Erwinna and heading uphill along Geigel Hill and Upper Tinicum Church roads. This climb isn't dramatically steep but it does last for several miles, leveling out as you reach Chestnut Ridge and Birch roads.

The route passes another county park on Ringing Rocks Road. The main feature of Ringing Rocks Park is a vast field of boulders reached by

Variation:

Shorten the ride by cutting across Perry Auger Rd. At mile 2.8 in the directions, bear left onto Perry Auger. Follow Perry Auger approximately two miles to the intersection with Stanley Rd. (mile 14.9 in the directions). Turn left to continue on Perry Auger and pick up the directions as written. This creates a ride of about 18 miles and preserves most of the interesting scenery on the route, although it doesn't eliminate the toughest hills.

a foot trail from the parking area. (See page 79 for more on the musical qualities of these big rocks.) You'll pass similar boulders by the side of the road all along this route, and there's a rather towering pile of them near the intersection of Beaver Run and Clay Ridge roads. This area also seems to have a disproportionate number of barking dogs and what you might be tempted to call mobile homes, except that it's clear they aren't going anywhere soon.

Another thing about this part of Bucks County: You might almost think it's too remote from civilization for proper mapmakers to have made it this far, which leads to a word of warning about using ordinary commercial maps to navigate in this area. Some of these roads seem to change name without warning, while in other places you'll find roads that seem to be separate yet have the same name. Particular care has been given to make sure the road names on the map in this book match the names on local signs (which are rare, anyway).

Most of the scenery on this ride is quite similar, but there's a nice view of some distant hills when you turn onto Geigel Hill Road from Beaver Run Road, and Sheep Hole Road is unpaved and travels along a pretty stream through an isolated valley.

Frenchtown, the nearest outpost of civilization, has a number of restaurants and art galleries and is a rather pleasant place to visit. You can get there via the bridge north of Tinicum Park.

The bridge between Frenchtown and Uhlerstown

Good to know:

Bridge Cafe, 8 Bridge St., Frenchtown, N.J., (908) 996-6040. A neat little casual restaurant located next to the River Rd. parking area in a former train station. There's a glassed-in dining room with a fine view of the river and the bridge.

Ringing Rocks Park, Ringing Rocks Rd., Bridgeton Township, (215) 757-0571 (Bucks County Parks Dept.). Picnicking, trail to rocks, scenic waterfalls, rest rooms.

Tinicum Park, Route 32 (River Rd.), Erwinna, (215) 757-0571 (Bucks County Parks Dept.). Picnicking, ball fields, camping, rest rooms.

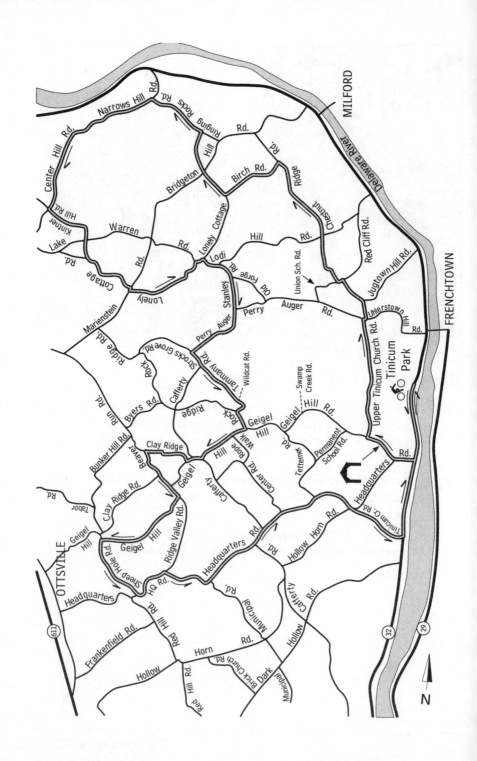

Directions:

0.0 Turn **right** from Tinicum Park onto Route 32 (River Rd.).

0.4 Turn **right** onto Headquarters Rd.

0.7 When Headquarters goes off to the left, go **straight** ahead onto Geigel Hill Rd.

0.8 Go through the covered bridge.

1.2 Turn **right** onto Upper Tinicum Church Rd.

2.8 When Perry Auger Rd. goes off to the left, bear **right** to stay on Upper Tinicum Church (you want the middle of three roads here; the hard right is Uhlerstown Hill Rd.).

3.6 When Red Cliff Rd. comes in from the right, stay **straight** on Upper Tinicum Church.

3.7 When Union School Rd. goes straight ahead at an intersection with a grassy triangle in the middle, turn **right** to stay on Upper Tinicum Church. (It becomes Chestnut Ridge Rd. after the intersection with Lodi Hill Rd.)

5.5 Turn **left** onto Birch Rd.

6.4 When Birch ends at a stop sign, turn **right** onto Lonely Cottage Rd.

6.9 At the stop sign, cross Bridgetown Hill Rd. and continue **straight** ahead on Lonely Cottage.

7.4 When Lonely Cottage ends at a stop sign, turn **left** onto Ringing Rocks Rd.

8.3 When Ringing Rocks ends at a stop sign, turn **left** onto Narrows Hill Rd. (it becomes Center Hill Rd.).

10.7 Turn **left** onto Kintner Hill Rd.

11.7 When Lonely Cottage comes in from the right, go **straight** ahead; you're now on Lonely Cottage.

12.6 At the stop sign at Marienstein Rd., go **right then left** to continue on Lonely Cottage.

13.6 At the intersection with Lake Warren Rd. on the left, turn **right** to continue on Lonely Cottage.

13.8 Turn **right** onto Lodi Hill Hill.

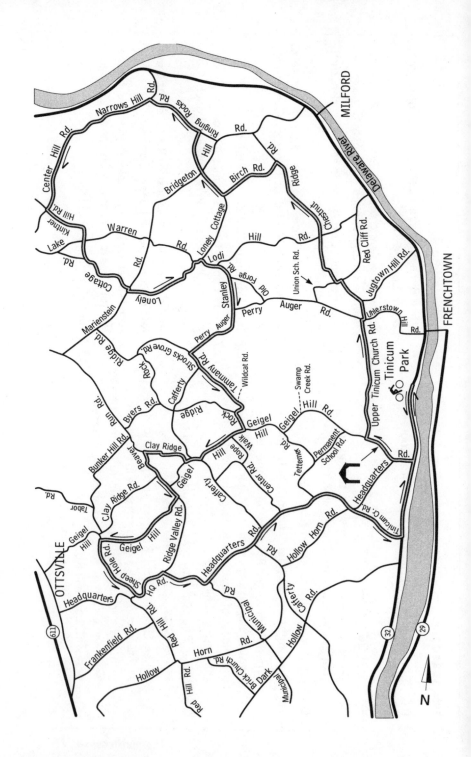

14.0 When Lodi Hill goes off to the left, turn **right** onto Old Forge Rd.

14.3 Turn **right** onto Stanley Rd.

14.9 At the stop sign where Perry Auger Rd. comes in from the left, go **straight** ahead onto Perry Auger.

15.8 At the stop sign where Strocks Grove Rd. goes off to the right, turn **left** onto Tammany Rd.

16.1 When Cafferty Rd. goes off to the right, stay **left** on Tammany Rd.

17.0 When Tammany ends at a stop sign, turn **left** onto Rock Ridge Rd.

17.3 When Rock Ridge ends at a stop sign, turn **right** onto Geigel Hill Rd.

18.2 Turn **right** onto Clay Ridge Rd.

18.7 When Clay Ridge ends at a stop sign, turn **left** onto Beaver Run Rd. (there's a huge pile of boulders on your right at this intersection).

19.7 Turn **right** onto Geigel Hill.

21.0 Just before the one-lane bridge at the bottom of the hill, turn **left** onto unpaved Sheep Hole Rd.

22.0 When Sheep Hole ends at a stop sign, turn **left** onto Headquarters Rd.

22.5 At the stop sign where Ridge Valley Rd. goes straight ahead, turn **right** to continue on Headquarters.

25.9 When Headquarters goes off to the left, go **straight** onto Tinicum Creek Rd.

26.7 Turn **left** onto Route 32.

28.1 Return to Tinicum Park on the **left.**

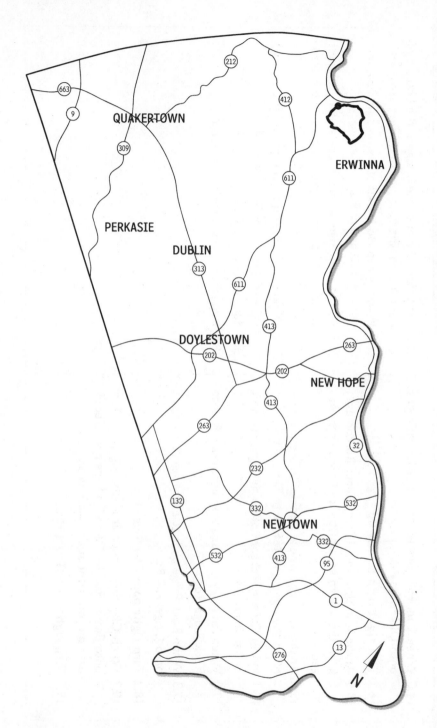

Ringing Rocks

Distance: 7.9 miles

Rating: Easy

Start: Ringing Rocks Park

This basically is a shorter and much easier version of the ride described in the previous chapter. It begins at Ringing Rocks Park and circles more or less around the top of a plateau, avoiding the steep hills that rise up to this area and make the longer ride difficult. However, this ride does include one sustained but not too steep climb on Narrows Hill Road and a steep but mercifully short hill on Lonely Cottage Road just north of Bridgeton Hill Road.

To find Ringing Rocks Park, take Route 32 to Bridgeton Hill Road, which is just north of the bridge to Milford, N.J. From Bridgeton Hill Road, turn right after the Bridgeton Elementary School onto Ringing Rocks Road. You'll see a sign for the park soon after the turn. There are picnic tables and rest rooms near the parking lot. At the far end of the lot from the entrance, two trails lead down to the natural feature for which the park was named: An eight-acre field of huge boulders, which present a truly amazing sight when you first come out of the woods and find them arrayed before you. Even more amazing is the fact that some of the boulders make a clear ringing noise when struck with a hammer. (Bring one along if you want to enjoy this feature of the park.)

The field of boulders was formed when erosion carried away most of the soil, leaving the big rocks behind. Only some of them ring. The best sounds are produced by the boulders that are suspended from other rocks in a way that allows them to vibrate. To find the ones that sound best, look for the marks left by the hammers of previous music makers. There are stories about people creating rocky bell choirs by finding boulders to sound every note in the scale, but you don't have to play a real tune to have fun here. Most people find this place fascinating because it's such a departure from the usual recreation area.

Outside of the park, the ride is pretty in an unexceptional sort of way. You'll see boulders like the ones in Ringing Rocks Park along the side of the road in some places, though there are no other big accumulations of these rocks. The route takes you mostly through wooded areas and through part of State Game Lands No. 56, which is popular with mountain bikers. (See page 105 for information on mountain biking in Bucks County). There are no towns or other attractions along this route.

Good to know:

Ringing Rocks Park, Ringing Rocks Rd., Bridgeton Township, (215) 757-0571 (Bucks County Parks Dept.). Picnicking, trail to rocks, scenic waterfalls, rest rooms.

A roadside boulder does duty as a bike rack

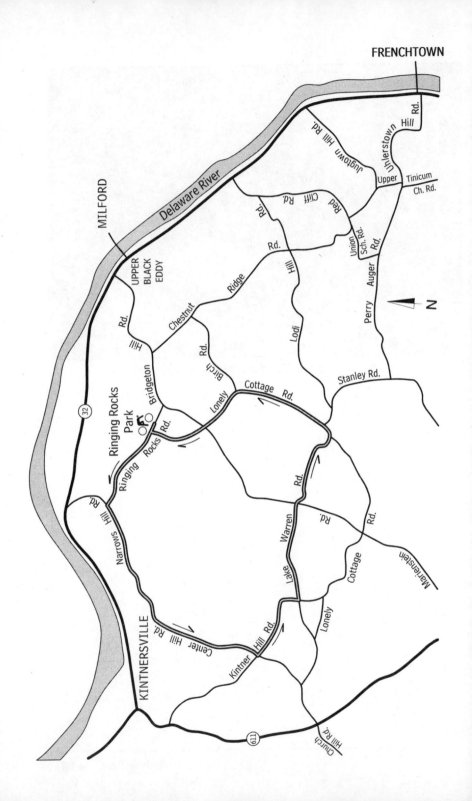

Directions:

0.0 Turn **right** from the parking lot at Ringing Rocks Park onto Ringing Rocks Rd.

0.9 When Ringing Rocks ends at a stop sign, turn **left** onto Narrows Hill Rd. (it becomes Center Hill Rd.).

3.2 Turn **left** onto Kintner Hill Rd.

4.0 Turn **left** onto Lake Warren Rd.

4.9 At the stop sign, cross Marienstein Rd. and continue **straight** ahead on Lake Warren.

5.7 When Lake Warren ends at a stop sign, turn **left** onto Lonely Cottage Rd.

7.2 At the stop sign, cross Bridgeton Hill Rd. and continue **straight** ahead on Lonely Cottage.

7.8 When Lonely Cottage ends at a stop sign, turn **right** onto Ringing Rocks.

7.9 Turn **left** to return to the parking lot at Ringing Rocks Park.

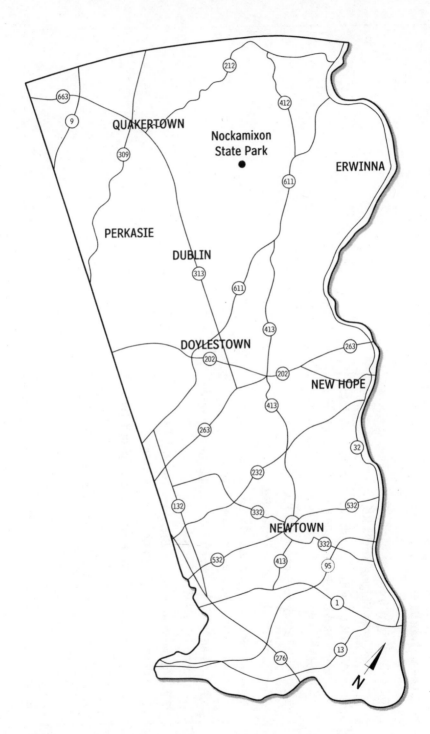

Nockamixon State Park

Distance: 2.8 miles
Rating: Easy
                Paved bike path

Nockamixon State Park encircles beautiful Lake Nockamixon, one of the prettiest places anywhere in Bucks County. There are parking and picnic areas scattered all around the lake, which is seven miles long. Its facilities emphasize boating but include a bicycle trail that is relatively short and easy, extending only 2.8 miles over rolling terrain that is suitable for all but the very youngest of bicycle riders.

Is it worth traveling all the way to this park to ride a 2.8-mile bike path? Quite possibly not, if cycling is the only thing you have in mind. However, the park is a good place to leave your car while you explore the area nearby (see page 89 for another ride starting from this park). And if you're looking for a family outing including a variety of outdoor activities, the other park facilities can make it worth your while.

Nockamixon has a boat rental concession that offers canoes, motorboats, rowboats, sailboats, pedalboats and pontoon boats. There are four boat launch areas for those who bring their own. The park also has a fishing pier, equestrian trails (no bikes allowed), lots of picnic tables, and a swimming pool with dressing rooms, a playground, and a snack bar. In addition, there's a family cabin area on the south shore of the lake where ten two- and three-bedroom cabins are available for rental.

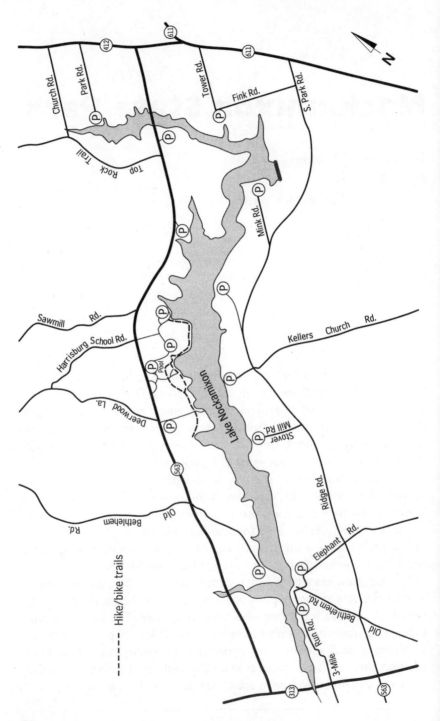

Lake Nockamixon

Hike/bike trails

Variation:

Ride on Route 563. If you want to extend your ride beyond the park bike path, try Route 563. It's rolling and carries a fair amount of traffic, but its shoulders are very wide and well-paved and are just fine for cycling.

The bike path begins by the water at the end of the marina by the main visitor center. It heads along the edge of the lake past the boat rental concession and ends at a little cove past the fishing pier. The path is somewhat winding and it's important not to pick up too much speed on the downhills, because you can never tell what lies around the next curve. Cyclists must also watch out for cars when crossing the extension of Deerwood Lane near the fishing pier. Another loop of the path goes up to the swimming pool.

Good to know:

Nockamixon State Park, 1542 Mountain View Dr., Quakertown, (215) 529-7300 or 1-800-63-PARKS. Boating, boat rentals, fishing, picnicking, bike path, equestrian trails, rest rooms, family cabins. Swimming pool; admission charged.

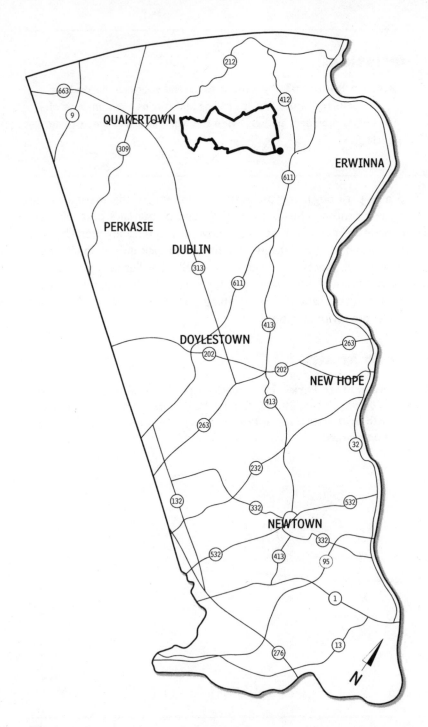

Haycock

Distance: 20.2 miles
Rating: Medium
Start: Nockamixon State Park

Although this ride skirts the base of Haycock Mountain (960 feet), it is mostly rolling as it meanders through the area north of Lake Nockamixon. If the weather is right and you're in the mood, you can finish the ride with a swim in the pool at Nockamixon State Park (see page 85 for more information on park facilities).

The route begins at the Haycock Boat Access, which is located at the far end of the park toward Route 611. If you take Routes 611 and 412 to get there, turn left onto Route 563 and you'll find it on the left a little less than a mile from 412. If you come from the other direction, it'll be on the right almost seven miles from Route 313. Be careful not to confuse the Haycock boat area with the Nockamixon Boat Access, which is located just west of it.

Like the Three-Mile Run Boat Access area used in the lakes ride on page 55, this one has nothing more than picnic tables, rest rooms, and plenty of parking, but on a fine summer day that can serve as an advantage, keeping you away from all the people who turn out to use the other areas of the park.

The ride begins on Route 563, which probably is the busiest road on the route but has a nice wide shoulder suitable for cycling. You soon turn onto Trap Rock Road, however, and follow some relatively untraveled roads around Haycock Mountain. Trap Rock is wooded at first as you pass the state game lands, but the scenery opens up a little as you come around to St. John the Baptist Church, an old building with a cemetery across the street.

It's mostly woods from here to Old Bethlehem Pike, which seems to divide the landscape in two parts, with woods mostly on the east side and open farmland to the west. You'll pass Lake Towhee Park, a big county facility, along the way. Its main entrance is on Old Bethlehem Pike, but you can get into the Lake Towhee Nature Center from Saw Mill Road.

The area between routes 313 and 611 north of the lake is peaceful but quite rural, and you won't find many places to stop along the way. The Parkway Drive In on Old Bethlehem Road is the one exception. It's a real reminder of times past, and worth a look if you have the time to spare.

Good to know:

Lake Towhee Park, Old Bethlehem Rd., Applebachsville, (215) 757-0571 (Bucks County Parks Dept.). Picnicking, playgrounds, ball fields, equestrian trails, boating, fishing, camping, nature area.

Parkway Drive In, Old Bethlehem and Thatcher rds., Quakertown, (215) 538-2904. An old-fashioned roadside restaurant complete with mini-golf course.

Variations:

Use Axe Handle Rd. to make the ride longer. To add about three miles and another stretch of pretty road to the ride, try this short detour on Axe Handle Rd.: At the intersection of Union and W. Thatcher rds. (mile 11.8), turn right onto W. Thatcher. Turn left onto Axe Handle, and left again in about a half a mile to continue on Axe Handle. Turn left onto Clymer Rd. and left onto Richlandtown Rd. From Richlandtown, turn right onto Covered Bridge Rd. and pick up the planned route at mile 13.2.

Shorten the route by cutting across Harrisburg School Rd. From Sawmill Rd. just after the turn from Stony Garden Rd. (mile 6.5), turn left onto Deerwood La. Turn left again onto Harrisburg School Rd. Turn left onto Route 563 and follow it back to the Haycock Boat Launch Access parking area. This makes a ride of about 11 miles.

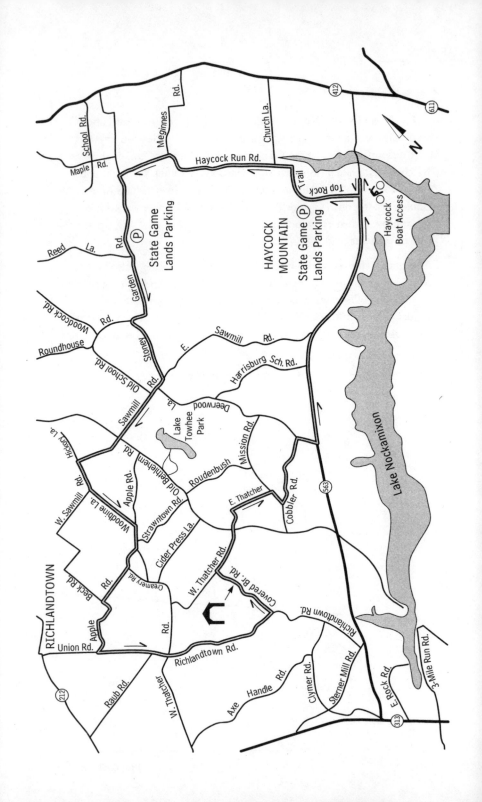

Directions:

0.0 Turn **left** onto Route 563 from the Haycock Boat Access parking area.

0.2 Turn **right** onto Top Rock Trail (there's a sign on the left for St. John the Baptist Church).

1.4 The road bends sharply to the left and becomes Haycock Run Rd.

3.7 When Haycock Run ends at a stop sign, turn **left** onto Stony Garden Rd.

5.7 When Roundhouse Rd. goes straight ahead, turn **left** to continue on Stony Garden.

6.5 When E. Sawmill Rd. comes in from the left, stay **straight** to continue on Sawmill.

7.4 At the stop sign, cross Old Bethlehem Rd. and continue **straight** ahead on W. Sawmill.

8.0 When Hickory La. comes in from the right, turn **left** to continue on Sawmill.

8.4 Turn **left** onto Woodbine Lane.

9.1 When Woodbine ends at a stop sign, turn **right** onto Apple Rd.

9.4 At the Y intersection, bear **right** to stay on Apple.

10.2 When Beck Rd. comes in from the right, turn **left** to stay on Apple.

10.9 When Apple ends at a stop sign, turn **left** onto Union Rd.

11.8 At the stop sign, cross W. Thatcher and continue **straight** ahead on Richlandtown Rd.

13.2 Turn **left** onto Covered Bridge Rd. (follow signs for the Tohickon Family Campground).

13.8 Go through the covered bridge.

14.1 When Covered Bridge ends at a stop sign, turn **right** onto W. Thatcher.

14.7 At the stop sign, cross Old Bethlehem Rd. and continue **straight** ahead on E. Thatcher.

15.4 When E. Thatcher ends at a stop sign, turn **right** onto Mission Rd.

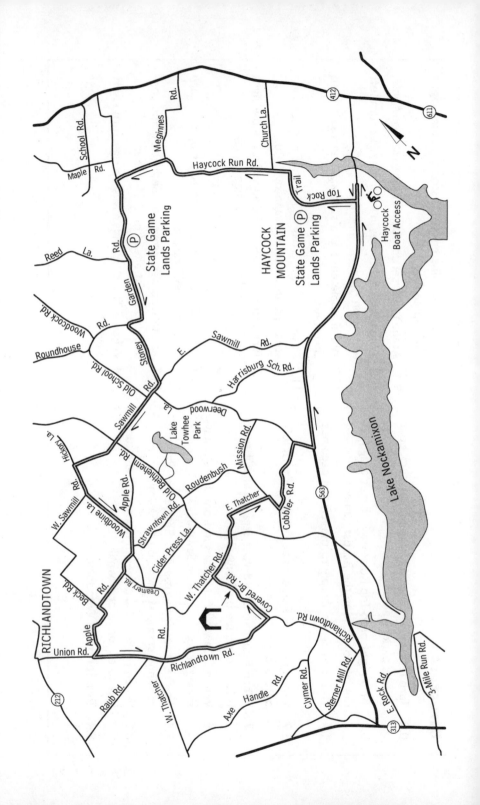

15.6 When Mission goes off to the right, turn **left** onto Cobbler Rd.

16.4 When Cobbler ends at a stop sign, turn **right** onto Deerwood La.

16.7 When Deerwood ends at a stop sign, turn **left** onto Route 563.

20.2 Return to the Haycock Boat Access.

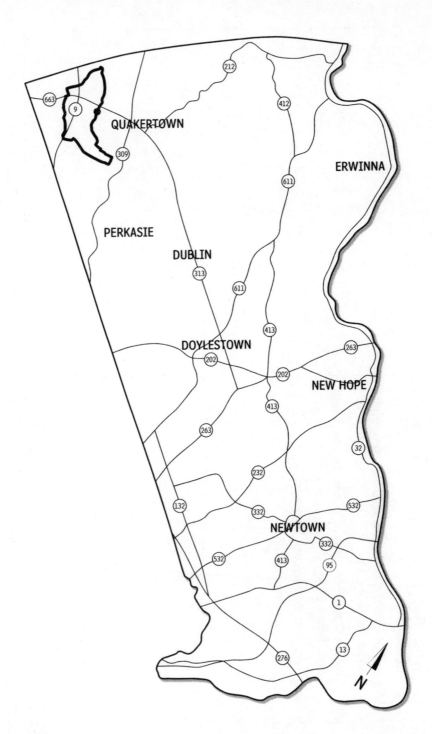

Trumbauersville

Distance: 16.9 miles
Rating: Medium
Start: Milford Township Park

Before I started searching out good roads to bike in places where I hadn't previously spent much time, I'd never heard of Trumbauersville and the smaller towns on this ride, places like Spinnerstown, Steinsburg, and Milford Square. It was my loss. Up here west of Quakertown, in the last corner of Bucks County before you cross the border toward Allentown, you'll find some really pretty cycling country.

The ride begins at the Milford Township Park just south of Unami Creek. The easiest way to find it is via Route 663 and Allentown Road. (Route 313 turns into Route 663 at the intersection with Route 309 in Quakertown.) If you're coming from Quakertown, turn left at Allentown Road (there's a light) and go through the town of Milford Center (there's a stop sign). Cross the one-lane bridge over Unami Creek, turn left at the end of the bridge onto Mill Road, and you're there.

Although there's a hill on the first part of Allentown Road, the terrain soon settles down to mostly rolling, and there are no drastic hills anywhere on this ride. You'll reach the town of Trumbauersville within a mile. Main Street (Allentown Road) and Broad Street are the center of town. In addition to a church, a coin laundry, a candy store, and a post

Variations:

Ride down Mill Rd. along Unami Creek. Take Mill Rd. away from Allentown Rd.; when you reach Creamery Rd. about a half mile later, turn around and ride back. This short detour into the Milford Township Park doesn't really go anywhere, but it's very pretty.

Check out the dam on Nursery Rd. off Trumbauersville Rd. To find it, skip the turn onto Canary Rd. at mile 7.4 and go about a quarter mile farther on Trumbauersville Rd. to Nursery Rd. Turn left onto Nursery. You'll cross a green metal bridge near a dam that creates a small pond on Unami Creek. There's a trail at the end of the bridge leading to the dam, a spot where children fish and swing their feet in the water.

office, it has a pizzeria (you'll pass it on Main Street) and a luncheonette (turn right on Broad).

After Trumbauersville, you're soon back in the country. There's a nice pond just before the start of Camp Rockhill Road and a very nice view of a ridge line from Esten Road. Canary Road takes you into the woods, and Brinkman Road brings you out into open farmland again. On the north of Route 663, just after you cross over from Brinkman, there's a view of a white church spire atop a hill that is reminiscent of some rural towns in Vermont.

Spinnerstown is another crossroads town, with a small convenience store where you can stop for a cold drink if you're so inclined. It's the last outpost of civilization on this ride; the views as you ride along Steinsburg Road from here will be of hills and distant mountains in Northampton County.

From Steinsburg, where you pick up Allentown Road again, it's a long downhill to the light at Route 663, and from there it's a relatively short ride back to the Milford Township Park.

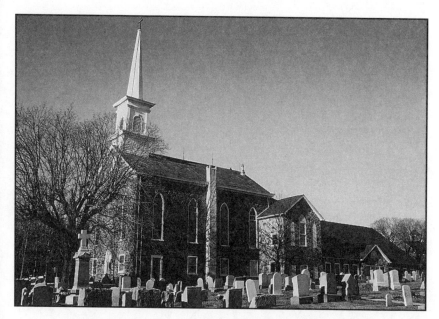

St. John's Evangelical Lutheran Church in Spinnerstown

Good to know:

Michael's Market, Spinnerstown and Steinsburg roads, Spinnerstown, (215) 538-1833. A convenience store located right on the ride route.

Pistone's Pizza, 14 N. Main St., Trumbauersville, (215) 529-9553. A pizzeria, also right on the route.

Spor's General Store, 22 W. Broad St., Trumbauersville, (215) 536-6754. A luncheonette and ice cream place, with soda machines outside. Find it by turning right onto Broad as you pass through Trumbauersville; it'll be on the left.

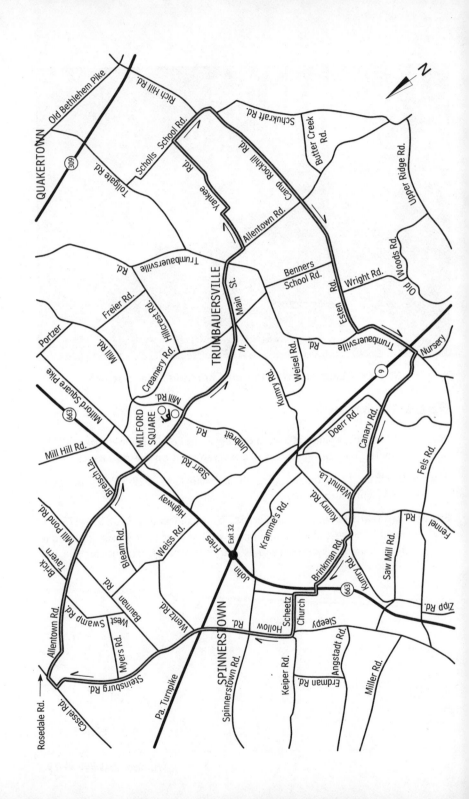

Directions:

0.0 From the Milford Township Park on Mill Rd., turn **left** onto Allentown Rd.

1.1 At the stop sign in Trumbauersville, stay **straight** to continue on Allentown (N. Main St.).

2.0 Turn **left** onto Yankee Rd.

3.4 When Yankee ends at a stop sign, turn **right** onto Scholls School Rd.

3.9 Follow Scholls School as it bends to the right and becomes Camp Rockhill Rd.

4.3 At a stop sign, cross Allentown Rd. and continue **straight** ahead on Esten Rd.

6.7 When Esten ends at a stop sign, turn **left** onto Trumbauersville Rd.

7.4 After crossing the Pennsylvania Turnpike, make the first **right** onto Canary Rd.

9.4 When Canary ends at a stop sign, turn **left** onto Kumry Rd.

9.5 Bear **right** onto Brinkman Rd.

10.2 At the stop sign, cross Route 663 (John Frees Hwy.) very carefully and continue **straight** ahead.

10.5 Turn **left** onto Scheetz Church Rd.

10.9 When Scheetz Church ends at a stop sign, turn **right** onto Sleepy Hollow Rd.

11.4 At the stop sign in Spinnerstown, cross Spinnerstown Rd. and continue **straight** ahead on Steinsburg Rd.

13.6 When Cassel Rd. comes in from the left, turn **right** onto Rosedale Rd.

13.7 At a four-way stop, turn **right** onto Allentown.

16.1 At the traffic signal, cross Route 663 and continue **straight** ahead on Allentown.

16.9 Turn **left** onto Mill to return to the parking area.

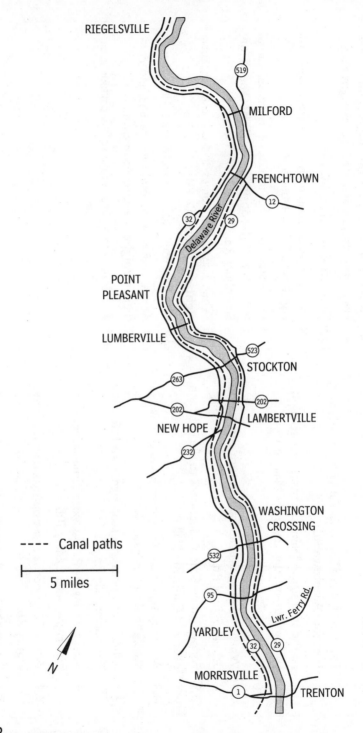

RIEGELSVILLE

519

MILFORD

FRENCHTOWN

12

32 Delaware River 29

POINT
PLEASANT

LUMBERVILLE

523

STOCKTON

263

202

202

NEW HOPE

LAMBERTVILLE

232

WASHINGTON
CROSSING

- - - - Canal paths

532

5 miles

95

Lwr. Ferry Rd.

YARDLEY

32 29

N

MORRISVILLE

1

TRENTON

The canals

If you love bicycling but hate cars and hills, the multi-use paths along the Delaware River might be just what you're looking for. They offer opportunities to ride extended distances without having to worry about traffic or steep climbs, and they are wonderful for families looking for a good place to ride together.

In Pennsylvania, the Delaware Canal runs all the way from Easton to Bristol, although it has been paved over in many places south of Morrisville. Unfortunately, the grass and dirt surface of this towpath leaves a lot to be desired. In some places there are rocks and roots embedded in the path, and occasionally it slopes rather precariously toward the water. It's too tame to serve for serious mountain biking, and too rough to be very pleasant for anyone else. There are plans for major improvements including construction of a better bicycle path from Morrisville to Uhlerstown within the next few years, but for now the canal in New Jersey is a far better place to take your bike.

On that side of the river, a former railroad right-of-way beside the Delaware & Raritan Canal has been covered with fine packed gravel that provides a fairly decent surface for cycling. This path runs all the way from Frenchtown to Lower Ferry Road in Ewing Township, although there's a gap of about a mile in Lambertville (between Bridge Street and the Holcombe Jimison Farmstead, just south of the Route 202 bridge over the Delaware). Cyclists who want to ride through must detour onto city streets, using Bridge Street, North Union Street, Cherry Street, and a short stretch of Route 29.

You can leave your car at Washington Crossing State Park, the Holcombe Jimison Farmstead at the north end of Lambertville, Prallsville Mills in Stockton, or the Bull's Island Recreation Area about three miles north of Stockton; all of these facilities are located on Route 29. The towns of New Hope, Lambertville, Stockton and Frenchtown make good places to stop for refreshments. You can use the Delaware River bridges at Morrisville, Washington Crossing, New Hope, Centre Bridge, Lumberville, or Uhlerstown to make a loop ride using the canals on both sides of the river.

Good to know:

See bike shop listings on page 107 for bicycle rental information.

Bull's Island Recreation Area, 2185 Daniel Bray Highway (Route 29) Stockton, N.J., (609) 397-2949. Hiking, camping, picnicking, rest rooms, access to Delaware & Raritan Canal and Delaware River. Pedestrian bridge to Lumberville in Pennsylvania.

Dilly's Corner, Routes 263 and 32, Centre Bridge, (215) 862-5333. A classic hamburger and ice cream stand near the bridge over the Delaware from Stockton. Use the steps from the canal towpath to the bridge.

Delaware Canal State Park, (610) 982-5560. A 60-mile park running the length of the Delaware Canal in Pennsylvania.

Delaware & Raritan Canal State Park, (732) 873-3050. An 80-mile park running beside the canal from Milford to Trenton to New Brunswick in New Jersey.

Holcombe Jimison Farmstead, Route 29, Lambertville. Blacksmith shop and farm buildings dedicated to preserving Hunterdon County's rural heritage. Entrance just south of the Route 202 bridge.

Prallsville Mills, Route 29, Stockton, N.J. (609) 397-3586. Restored mill buildings, access to Delaware & Raritan Canal and Delaware River.

Washington Crossing State Park, Routes 29 & 546, Washington Crossing, N.J., (609) 737-0623. Picnicking, camping, hiking, nature center, visitor center, historic buildings, rest rooms, adjacent to Delaware & Raritan Canal and Delaware River.

Washington Crossing Historic Park, Routes 32 & 532, Washington Crossing, Pa., (215) 493-4076. Museum, historic buildings, picnicking, rest rooms, hiking.

Mountain biking

Ask a serious mountain biker about the best places for off-road riding in Bucks County, and you're likely to be told about the Wissahickon Valley and Pennypack Park in Philadelphia and the town of Jim Thorpe in Carbon County—none of which is actually in Bucks County. But that doesn't mean there's no place at all to ride around here.

The Delaware Canal towpath is obvious, if a little uninspiring. Thanks to the decrepit character of the canal in general, the towpath has become technically challenging in some places. On the whole, however, what we are talking about here is sixty miles of flat trail. The most popular places for off-road riding in Bucks County are at Ralph Stover State Park near Point Pleasant and on trails in the state game lands in northern Bucks, especially State Game Lands Nos. 157 and 56.

Ralph Stover is located on the Tohickon Creek and includes both a creek-level area and the section called High Rocks, a sheer cliff that rises 200 feet from the creek. The two areas are not adjacent but are connected by Bucks County's Tohickon Valley Park. The loop of seven to nine miles of trail through the two parks is highly technical in terms of rocks and logs across the way—and it obviously includes some respectable inclines. To reach the park, take Tohickon Hill Road and State Park Road from Route 32 in Point Pleasant, or Stump Road from Route 413.

The state game lands are administered by the Pennsylvania Game Commission and are scattered across northern Bucks County. They show up on most maps of the area. A more detailed topographic map of all four of the game lands in Bucks County is available from Alfred B. Patton in Doylestown. The ones used most by cyclists are State Game Lands No. 157 in Haycock Township and State Game Lands No. 56 in Tinicum, Nockamixon, and Bridgeton townships.

State Game Lands No. 157 includes Haycock Mountain north of Lake Nockamixon. It offers some excellent views, especially when the leaves are down from the trees. The entrance to the section used most by cyclists is from Top Rock Trail, but there is also parking off Stony Garden Road and Sawmill Road. (See page 92 for a map of this area.)

State Game Lands No. 56 is divided into six separate parcels that are connected in some places by trails and unpaved roads. Wildcat Road off Tettemer Road is a popular place to begin. (See page 74 for a map of this area.) From the parking area on Wildcat, the trail soon leads past a small lake. You can also ride from Swamp Creek Rd.

Some cyclists complain that these trails are not well marked. You should keep in mind, too, that the state game lands were acquired primarily for hunting. The main hunting season in Pennsylvania runs from September through February, but there is the possibility of encountering hunters at any time of the year. The game commission recommends wearing bright colors when using the game lands trails.

Good to know:

Alfred B. Patton, Swamp Rd. and Center St., Doylestown, Pa. 18901, (215) 345-0700. Ask for the map called Bucks County Pennsylvania State Game Lands.

Pennsylvania Game Commission, Southeast Region, RD 2, Box 2584, Reading, Pa. 19605, (800) 228-0791.

Ralph Stover State Park, 6011 State Park Rd., Pipersville, (610) 982-5560 or 1-800-63-PARKS. Hiking, picnicking, family cabins.

Tohickon Valley Park, Cafferty Rd., Tinicum Twp., (215) 757-0571 (Bucks County Parks Dept.). Hiking, fishing, camping, ball fields. Swimming pool; admission charged.

Bike shops & rentals

Bensalem: *Andalusia Bicycle Shop*, 1567 Bristol Pike, (215) 639-2022.

Bristol: A.B.C., 443 Mill St., (215) 785-2779. Repairs, all brands, parts, adult trikes, tandems, trailers, mountain bikes, BMX. Open Sun., Mon, Thurs, Fri. Bike trails.

Doylestown: *Bike Line of Doylestown*, 73 Old Dublin Pike, (215) 348-8015.

Cycle Sports Ltd., 641 N. Main St., (215) 340-2526. Custom fitting, custom frames & bikes, express service available, family and road bikes and accessories; full service, inventory store. (http://www.cyclesports.com)

Feasterville: *Guy's Bicycles*, 326 E. Street Rd., (215) 355-1166. Full service, custom fittings, road and off-road, plus hybrids. Pro shop on 2nd floor.

Levittown: *Bike Line*, 1355 E. Lincoln Hwy., (215) 547-7460. Bicycles, fitness equipment, repairs.

Lumberville: *Lumberville Store & Gallery*, 3744 River Rd., (215) 297-5388. Bicycle rentals.

Morrisville: *Bike King*, 364 W. Trenton Ave., (215) 736-3350. (http://www.bikeking.com.)

New Hope: *New Hope Cyclery*, 186 Old York Rd., (215) 862-6888. Bike rentals available. Bike sales, service and accessories. Skateboard sales.

Newtown: *Newtown Bicycle & Fitness*, 30 N. State St., (215) 968-3200. Active bicycle racer and tourist on staff. Very familiar with Bucks County roads.

Ottsville: *Freeman's Bicycle Shop*, 4105 Durham Rd., (610) 847-5506, also 52 Bridge St., Frenchtown, N.J., (908) 996-7712. Full service bicycle shop. Large selection of bikes, parts, accessories, and clothing. Rentals.

Stockton, N.J.: *Bike Depot*, 10 Bridge St., (609) 397-3637. Bicycle rentals at a location on the canal path in New Jersey, just across the Delaware from Centre Bridge, Pa.

Bike clubs & tourism

Bike clubs:

BKR Racing & Cycling Club, 364 W. Trenton Ave., Morrisville, Pa. 19067. Primarily a racing club, with rides at the A & B level. Annual dues: $50. (http://www.bikeking.com)

Central Bucks Bike Club, P.O. Box 295, Buckingham, Pa. 18912. Primarily oriented toward bike touring, CBBC sponsors weekend rides at all levels. Annual dues: $15. Best-known ride: Covered Bridges. (http://cbbc.cycle.org)

Suburban Cyclists Unlimited, P.O. Box 401, Horsham, Pa., 19044. Also primarily a touring club, SCU sponsors rides that roll through Bucks and Montgomery counties from Hatboro-Horsham High School each weekend. Annual dues: $12. Best-known rides: Lake Nockamixon and Mexican Metric. (http://www.fitforum.com/scu1.htm)

Tourism:

Bucks County is a popular weekend getaway destination, with many wonderful inns and restaurants eager to pamper visitors. Some offer special bicycling packages for those interested in touring the area on two wheels. These agencies can help you plan a visit:

Bucks County Conference & Visitors Bureau, 152 Swamp Rd., Doylestown PA 18901, (215) 345-4552, (800) 836-2825, fax (215) 345-4967. (http://www.bctc.org)

New Hope Borough Information Center, South Main and Mechanic sts., New Hope, (215) 862-5880.

Keep in touch

Do you have a favorite back roads bike ride of your own? Was there anything you especially liked (or didn't like) about one of the rides in this book? We'd like to know what you think. You can send a letter or e-mail.

Please share your thoughts about these routes. Tell us if road conditions have changed, or if you have corrections to any of the directions or listings. Let us know if you discovered any noteworthy watering holes or things to do not mentioned in this book.

Also, tell us about your own favorite bicycling routes. (They don't have to be in Bucks County.) Rides suggested by readers may be included in future editions of this or other bicycle tour books.

Please send your comments and suggestions to:

Freewheeling Press
P.O. Box 540
Lahaska PA 18931

You can also reach us via e-mail:
ckerr@voicenet.com

You can find useful information about bicycling in Bucks County and keep up with what's happening here at Freewheeling Press by visiting our Web site:

Bike New Hope
http://www.voicenet.com/~ckerr

Buy a book

It's easy to order one of Freewheeling Press's acclaimed bicycle tour books by mail. Use this form to get a copy of this book for a friend, or treat yourself to our guide to short scenic rides near the Delaware River in Bucks and Hunterdon counties. *The Back Roads Bike Book: A dozen scenic rides in and around Lambertville, N.J. and New Hope, Pa.* features relatively easy rides ranging in length from 5.7 to 14.7 miles and includes listings for nearby places to stay.

Name: _____

Address: _____

_____

_____

Telephone: _____

No.	Title	Price	Total
	Back Roads Bicycling in Bucks County, Pa.	$12.95	
	The Back Roads Bike Book	$12.95	

Send to:	Subtotal	
Freewheeling Press	Shipping ($2 per book)	
PO Box 540	Pa. residents add 6% tax	
Lahaska PA 18931	**Grand total**	
	Make check payable to Freewheeling Press	